The New York Times

Guide to
Finance

Jamie Murphy, Ph.D.
Department of Information
Management and Marketing
University of Western Australia

Iain Watson, Ph.D.
Department of Accounting and Finance
University of Western Australia

J. Brannen Murphy, DVM
Founding Chair of First Seminole State Bank

South-Western College Publishing
Thomson Learning™

Australia • Canada • Denmark • Japan • Mexico • New Zealand • Philippines
Puerto Rico • Singapore • South Africa • Spain • United Kingdom • United States

The New York Times Guide to Finance, by Jamie Murphy & Iain Watson

Publisher: Dave Shaut
Acquisitions Editor: Pamela M. Person
Marketing Manager: Rob Bloom
Production Editor: Elizabeth A. Shipp
Media and Technology Editor: Kevin von Gillern
Media Production Editor: Robin K. Browning
Manufacturing Coordinator: Sandee Milewski
Internal Design: Joe Devine
Cover Design: Joe Devine
Copyeditor: Brian L. Massey
Production House: Trejo Production
Printer: Webcom

    Printed in Canada
    1 2 3 4 5 03 02 01 00

For more information contact South-Western College Publishing, 5101 Madison Road, Cincinnati, Ohio, 45227 or find us on the Internet at http://www.swcollege.com
For permission to use material from this text or product, contact us by
• **telephone: 1-800-730-2214**
• **fax: 1-800-730-2215**
• **web: http://www.thomsonrights.com**

Library of Congress Cataloging-in-Publication Data
Murphy, Jamie.
    The New York times guide to finance / Jamie Murphy, Iain Watson, J. Brannen Murphy.
    p. cm.
    ISBN 0-324-04158-6 (alk. paper)
    1. Finance. I. Watson, Iain. II. Murphy, J. Bannen III. New York times.
    IV. Title.
HG173 .M87 2000
332.024--dc21   00-026315

This book is printed on acid-free paper.

P R E F A C E

The New York Times Guide to Finance is designed for students, professors and business professionals—anyone interested in staying current in business today. A collection of the best finance-related articles from the *New York Times*, this guide does more than inform: it also provides context for the effects of change on all aspects of business. Also included are articles from *CyberTimes*, the online-only technology section of the *New York Times on the Web*. Each article was selected for its relevance to today's business world.

In purchasing **The New York Times Guide to Finance,** you are not only purchasing the contents between the covers, but also unlimited access, via password, to related *New York Times* articles. Current articles will be linked from the South-Western College Publishing/*New York Times* Web site (http://nytimes.swcollege.com) on an ongoing basis as news breaks.

This guide can be used formally in the classroom or informally for life-long learning. All articles are accompanied by exploratory exercises and probing questions developed by experts in the field. Previews provide context for each chapter of articles and link them to key finance principles. This guide is divided into six sections organized to highlight critical factors in finance today. This organization allows for easy integration into any finance course.

Chapter 1: The Field of Finance. This opening chapter explores how the three major areas of finance (1) corporate, (2) financial markets and institutions and (3) investment analysis intertwine with the individual. Topics include: valuation principles, corporate governance, corporate finance, investment analysis, financial markets and financial institutions.

Chapter 2: Financial Institutions and Monetary Policy. Banks, the Federal Reserve, insurance companies, mortgage markets and others provide much of the economic force behind a global economy. Topics include: commercial banks, regulation, mortgage markets, interest rates, debt, monetary theory, monetary policy, the Federal Reserve and insurance.

Chapter 3: Technology's Impact on Finance. Computers and the Internet are rapidly reshaping the world of finance. Topics include: day trading, online trading, encryption, Internet taxation, chat rooms and electronic services.

Chapter 4: Financial Management in the Corporate Environment. At the corporate level, financial managers walk a fine line, balancing the interests of the board of directors, stockholders, customers and employees. Topics include: bankruptcy, short- and long-term financial planning, pension planning, venture capital, mergers and acquisitions.

Chapter 5: Personal Finance and Investment Management. Money, money, money. This chapter examines how individuals can earn it, keep it and invest it to make it grow. Topics include: entrepreneurship, personal finance, investment management, retirement, mutual funds, financial protection and financial security.

Chapter 6: Finance Today. Topics include: e-commerce, Y2K, fraud, money laundering, globalization, international finance and financial crises.

PEDAGOGICAL FEATURES

Critical Thinking Questions challenge you to form your own opinion about current topics. These questions can be used to stimulate classroom discussion or as the basis for formal assignments.

Story-specific Questions highlight important points from each story.

Short Application Assignments work well as hands-on exercises for both classroom discussion and formal assignments. Most assignments should take no more than a few hours to complete. Typical assignments include developing presentations and writing brief memos, reports, executive summaries and articles for company newsletters.

Building Research Skills exercises allow you to expand upon what you have learned from the *New York Times'* articles and explore the unlimited resources available to enhance your understanding of current events. Typical assignments include presentations, writing essays and building Web pages.

ADDITIONAL ONLINE PEDAGOGY

Sample Exercises provide examples for you to follow in completing assignments.

Additional Readings link to more than 100 additional stories, categorized by chapter, for further research.

Featured Sections are in-depth collections of stories on specific topics such as Social Security, Outlook 2000, The World Financial Crisis, Russia in Turmoil, Asia's Financial Crisis, The Euro and the New Europe, The Federal Reserve, Retirement, the U.S. Budget, Welfare, Looking Back at the Crash of '29, Quarterly Mutual Fund Report and Is Microsoft a Monopoly.

Book Reviews cover about 80 computer and digital technology books reviewed by the *New York Times*, listed alphabetically by author and linked to the original review.

ACKNOWLEDGMENTS

My sincere appreciation goes to co-authors, Drs. Iain Watson and J. Brannen Murphy, for their prompt feedback and guidance in helping to select stories and craft the pedagogy. Special recognition for patience and understanding goes to the editors with whom I've had the opportunity to work. They are Dr. Brian L. Massey, Nanyang Technological University, Singapore; Rob Fixmer and John Haskins, the *New York Times*; Jason Fry, the *Wall Street Journal*; Glenn Withiam, the *Cornell Hotel and Restaurant Administration Quarterly*; and Margaret Leonard, the *Florida State Times*.

This pioneering publishing project would not have been possible without the progressive thinking of the *New York Times* (Mike Levitas, Hilda Cosmo, Melanie Rosen, Christine M. Thompson, John Haskins and Jim Mones) and South-Western College Publishing (Pamela Person, Dave Shaut, Libby Shipp and Kevin von Gillern).

On a personal note, thanks to my lovely wife, Debbie, for her encouragement; my rambunctious children, Casey and Jamie, for letting me work in peace; my parents, Joan and Brannen, for their support; and my cyber-colleagues, Drs. Charles F. Hofacker, C. Edward Wotring, Edward J. Forrest, and Dick Mizerski for their inspiration.

C O N T E N T S

The Field of Finance

PREVIEW

The opening chapter introduces the study and practice of finance by focusing on how three financial areas—investment analysis, financial markets and corporate finance—intertwine with the individual. As the articles illustrate, classic and contemporary forces influence the field of finance.

In "For Value Investors, a History Lesson," Mark Hulbert argues that a stock's past market movements help predict its future movements. Technical analysis, as the article explains, "can help keep a value investor from stubbornly fighting the market for years on end."

The Dow Jones industrial average, however, keeps distancing itself from the past. Once again, this venerable stock market index has shed itself of tired, old industrial stocks in favor of younger technology stocks, as Floyd Norris explains in "After Its Latest Facelift, a Younger, Sexier Dow."

While adding technology stocks may seem like an easy fix for the Dow, valuing technology stocks—for example, Internet retailers—is an evolving mix of art and science. Leslie Kaufman examines a less-than-optimistic formula for analyzing Internet retailers in "Some Analysts Cut Through Fog of Growth for Net Retailers."

Compared to technology, the board of directors is a more down to earth influence on corporate finance. Although deadwood directors are far from an endangered species, as Sana Siwolop illustrates in "How Boards Deal With Lazy Directors," recent corporate initiatives are aimed at keeping boards fresh and involved.

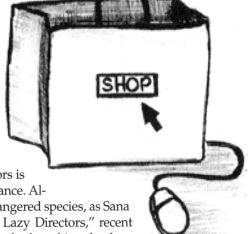

Source: Christine M. Thompson/CyberTimes

For Value Investors, a History Lesson

By Mark Hulbert

"In the long run, we're all dead," John Maynard Keynes once said. And many investors may want to similarly dismiss their value-oriented financial advisers, who often admonish them to shun the high-priced stocks that have led the market to new highs and, instead, focus on shares that are cheap on the basis of fundamentals.

Sure, these investors think, a company's stock price will *eventually* reflect its earnings and book value. But how long are they supposed to wait for those so-called value stocks to climb?

I have a suggestion for such investors: Try supplementing your value investing with technical analysis, which focuses on historical patterns of a stock's price and trading volume. In contrast to value advisers, who look at how the market ought to behave, technicians examine how it *does* behave. Technical analysis can help keep a value investor from stubbornly fighting the market for years on end.

There are many types of technical analysis, but the most basic tools are known as "support" and "resistance" levels. A stock's support level is the price from which previous rallies have sprung; a technically inclined investor who misses one rally will be inclined to buy the stock if it falls back to the support level. Enough such buying, of course, makes it difficult for the stock to fall beneath that level.

Conversely, a stock's resistance is the price where previous rallies have failed. Technically minded owners of a stock who didn't sell at the peak of a previous rally will be likely to sell if the stock rebounds to that price. With enough selling pressure, a stock will have difficulty penetrating its resistance level.

Many value investors may find all this sacrilegious. For years, such investors—who are focused on fundamentals—have ridiculed technical analysis as little better than reading tea leaves. Yet several academic studies have shown that there is something to it.

The best known of these was published in 1992 by the professors William Brock and Blake LeBaron of the University of Wisconsin and Josef Lakonishok of the University of Illinois. They tested various strategies that bought stocks at or near their support levels and sold them at or near their resistance levels. After the professors back-tested their strategies over 90 years, they concluded that technical analysis can beat the market. Other studies have found that technical analysis works in other markets as diverse as commodity futures and foreign currencies.

Technical analysis has vindicated itself outside the ivory tower, too. Every week since December 1983, the Value Line Investment Survey has published a technical ranking of 1,700 popular stocks.

This technical ranking system, whose exact methodology is proprietary, is different than the system for which Value Line is famous—a nontechnical one that has successfully used earnings and price momentum to gauge stocks' prospects.

According to Value Line's internal calculations, not only has its technical ranking system beaten the market over the last 15 years—by 6.1 percentage points a year, on average, not accounting for commissions, it has performed even better than its flagship stock-ranking system.

Technical analysis works because of investor psychology. Keynes once likened investing to guessing which contestant will win a beauty pageant. You don't pick the contestant you think is the most beautiful, but instead the one that you think the judges will choose. Similarly, a successful investor won't bet on companies he thinks the market *should* value highly, but instead on those that he thinks the market *will* value highly.

Investors needn't give up on their value approach to incorporate technical analysis. I believe the strategies can complement each other. If a value investor wants to cut his stock exposure, for example, then he should sell only those stocks that are near their resistance levels. Or, choosing between two value stocks that appear to be equally good bets, he could buy the one that is closest to its support level.

The New York Time, August 29, 1999
http://www.nytimes.com/library/financial/sunday/082999invest-strategies.html

CRITICAL THINKING QUESTIONS

1. Could one use technical analysis to invest successfully? Why, or why not?
2. What are the advantages and disadvantages of technical investing?
3. What are the advantages and disadvantages of value investing?
4. What weight should one give to technical versus value investing? Why?

STORY-SPECIFIC QUESTIONS

1. What is the difference between value analysis and technical analysis?
2. What are the two most basic tools of technical analysis?
3. In addition to the stock market, studies have shown that technical analysis works in various other markets. What two other markets does the story mention?
4. Briefly explain the following, "Technical analysis works because of investor psychology."

SHORT APPLICATION ASSIGNMENTS

1. In teams or individually, answer the story-specific questions; keep your answers to 25–75 words for each question.

2. In teams of three to five persons each, or as a whole class, discuss your responses to the critical thinking questions.
3. Prepare a one-page memo report (200–250 words) to your instructor in which you summarize this article. You will find a model one-page report on the Web site (nytimes.swcollege.com)
4. Write an executive summary (200–250 words). As an administrative assistant to a busy executive, you are expected to summarize selected articles and present important points. You will find a model executive summary on the Web site.
5. Summarize this article (100–125 words) for your company's newsletter. You will find a model newsletter article on the Web site.
6. Using a stock assigned by your instructor, or one of your own choosing, calculate the stock's hypothetical support and resistance level. Your instructor may ask you to present your findings in an oral report or submit a 150- to 200-word summary.

BUILDING RESEARCH SKILLS

1. Individually or in teams, investigate the Value Line Web site (http://www.valueline.com/index.html). What services are free? What services are not free? How would this site help the technical investor? Value investor? Your instructor may ask you to submit a three- to five-page essay, post a Web page or report your results in a five-minute presentation, along with a letter of transmittal explaining your findings.
2. Individually or in teams, research at least two technical analysis methods. Apply those methods to at least two stocks and make recommendations based on your technical analysis. Your instructor may ask you to submit a three- to five-page proposal, post a Web page or report your results in a five-minute presentation, along with a letter of transmittal explaining your proposal.
3. Using at least three other references (e.g., books, research-journal articles, newspaper or magazine stories or credible Web sites), write an 800- to 1,000-word essay that addresses two of the critical thinking questions offered earlier. Assume that your essay will be used as an internal reference for a financial institution's investment guidelines.
4. Using at least three other references (e.g., books, research-journal articles, newspaper or magazine stories or credible Web sites), post an 800- to 1,000-word Web page that addresses at least two of the earlier critical thinking questions. Assume that your page will be posted in the investment section of a corporate intranet.

After Its Latest Facelift, a Younger, Sexier Dow

By Floyd Norris

The Dow Jones industrial average has long been viewed as the most prominent measure of the financial health of corporate America. Maybe now it should be seen as a barometer of how fast the economy is changing.

Last week the keepers of the Dow—the editors of *The Wall Street Journal*—announced plans to boot four perfectly respectable companies and replace them with younger and better-performing substitutes. It was the third time in the 1990s that such a thing had happened. All told, 11 of the 30 stocks in the Dow are new in this decade.

To find any comparable rate of change one must return to the 1930s, when the Depression-era economy was suffering a very difficult upheaval. Now Wall Street thinks the economy is going through an upheaval with implications every bit as great—but much more pleasant—for the economy.

The old economy, as reflected in the Dow industrials of 20 years ago, was dominated by companies that made things—steel, cars, cigarettes, chemicals, oil and tires. The new Dow is dominated by companies in far different lines of work.

The Dow of the 1970s had three oil companies, two steel companies, one computer company and no financial firms. The new Dow has four computer-related companies, three financial behemoths, just one oil company and no steel makers. It has Walt Disney, Coca-Cola and McDonald's. But Alcoa is still on the list, and so are General Motors and Minnesota Mining and Manufacturing. The old America of heavy industry is still represented, but not nearly as heavily.

One sign of the magnitude of the change is that of the four companies that will join the Dow tomorrow, three of them—Intel, Microsoft and Home Depot—can trace their corporate lineage no further back than 1968. The fourth, SBC Communications, was spun off by AT&T (another Dow member) back in 1984 as part of the antitrust settlement that broke up Ma Bell. The companies they replaced—Chevron, Sears, Goodyear and Union Carbide—all joined the Dow in 1930 or earlier.

It's hard to underestimate the symbolic power of the Dow. Intel and Microsoft are emblematic of American dominance in the rapidly growing personal computer business. That image is better than the one created in 1985, when McDonald's joined the index, or in 1991, when USX, the former U.S. Steel, was tossed out to make way for Disney. Then there was talk that the new America meant hamburger flippers going to movies.

In announcing the changes, Paul E. Steiger, *The Journal*'s managing editor, spoke of making the Dow "more representative of the emerging U.S. economy." But he also evidently wanted to stick to blue chips, companies that had proven themselves to be successful. There are no pure Internet companies in the Dow.

The pace of change in the Dow may reflect more than the speed of change in the economy. After all, the economy was changing from the 1940s through the early 1980s, even though there were few changes in the Dow during that period that were not forced by takeovers or financial distress.

One thing that is different now is that Dow Jones & Company makes money from fees paid every time investors buy options, futures and other securities based on the Dow. In recent years, the index has not risen as fast as its prime competitor, the Standard & Poor's 500, which includes 500 major American stocks and has a very heavy dose of technology stocks and a larger share of the market in stock index securities.

Had Intel, Microsoft, Home Depot and SBC Communications been part of the Dow since 1997, the index would have been the better performer. Perhaps such superior performance would have persuaded more investors to trade the Dow, rather than the S&P.

The New York Times, October 31, 1999
http://www.nytimes.com/library/review/103199dow-review.html

CRITICAL THINKING QUESTIONS

1. Should the Dow Jones industrial average be viewed as the most prominent measure of the financial health of corporate America? Why, or why not?
2. Should the Dow Jones industrial average be updated as frequently as it has been in the last decade? Why, or why not?
3. What other major indexes, besides the Dow, should one follow? Why?
4. Are the recent changes driven by the fact that Dow Jones & Company makes money from fees paid every time investors buy options, futures and other securities based on the Dow? Why, or why not?

STORY-SPECIFIC QUESTIONS

1. Who are the keepers of the Dow?
2. How many stocks are in the Dow Jones industrial average?
3. What types of companies dominated to old economy, or the Dow industrials of 20 years ago?
4. What four companies joined the Dow? Left the Dow?

SHORT APPLICATION ASSIGNMENTS

1. In teams or individually, answer the story-specific questions; keep your answers to 25–75 words for each question.
2. In teams of three to five persons each, or as a whole class, discuss your responses to the critical thinking questions.
3. Prepare a one-page memo report (200–250 words) to your instructor in which you summarize this article. You will find a model one-page report on the Web site (nytimes.swcollege.com)
4. Write an executive summary (200–250 words). As an administrative assistant to a busy executive, you are expected to summarize selected articles and present important points. You will find a model executive summary on the Web site.
5. Summarize this article (100–125 words) for your company's newsletter. You will find a model newsletter article on the Web site.
6. In teams or individually, investigate which stocks comprise the Dow Jones industrial average. When was the last time this average changed? Your instructor may ask you to present your findings in an oral report or submit a 150- to 200-word summary.

BUILDING RESEARCH SKILLS

1. Individually or in teams, investigate the Dow Jones Web site (http://dowjones.wsj.com/p/main.html). What services are free? What services are not free? How would this site help the individual investor? Institutional investor? Your instructor may ask you to submit a three- to five-page essay, post a Web page or report your results in a five-minute presentation, along with a letter of transmittal explaining your findings.
2. Individually or in teams, compare the Dow Jones industrial average with at least three other indices, such as the NASDAQ or S&P 500. Your comparison could include each index's performance, composition, weighting and rate of change. Your instructor may ask you to submit a three- to five-page proposal, post a Web page or report your results in a five-minute presentation, along with a letter of transmittal explaining your proposal.
3. Using at least three other references (e.g., books, research-journal articles, newspaper or magazine stories or credible Web sites), write an 800- to 1,000-word essay that addresses two of the critical thinking questions offered earlier. Assume that your essay will be used as an internal reference for a financial institution's investment guidelines.
4. Using at least three other references (e.g., books, research-journal articles, newspaper or magazine stories or credible Web sites), post an 800- to 1,000-word Web page that addresses at least two of the earlier critical thinking questions. Assume that your page will be posted in the investment section of a corporate intranet.

Some Analysts Cut Through Fog of Growth for Net Retailers

By Leslie Kaufman

Financial reports from Internet retailers are like the pronouncements of the Delphic Priestess: future focused and infamously inscrutable.

Traditional retailers, Sears and Wal-Mart among them, report changes in sales for stores open at least one year, providing analysts a way to evaluate whether growth is real or merely a construct of new stores.

Online merchants offer no such equivalent.

Amazon.com, the king of E-tailers, reports skyrocketing revenues each quarter. But the numbers include income from newly acquired businesses, leaving outsiders no way to discern whether the core book business is driving the growth or whether income from the new additions masks a decline there. (In his most recent quarterly call with investors Amazon's founder and chief executive Jeff Bezos, said revenue was growing across all parts of the business, but declined to give specifics. His remarks put pressure on the stock, which has fallen 40 percent from its peak in April but remains up 16 percent for the year.)

Since most Wall Street analysts who follow Internet retailers work for firms grown fat on taking these companies public, there is little incentive to complain. But a small group of renegade skeptics has taken on the task of clearing the fog and are applying their approach to companies besides Amazon. Their method is simple—perhaps deceptively so. They are taking the two numbers that E-tailers love to trumpet (because they are always growing) total revenues for a quarter and total customer base and dividing one by the other. The results are eyebrow raising. They go straight down.

Eric Von der Porten, who runs a small hedge fund in San Carlos, California, has crunched the numbers for Amazon and CDNow, the online music store rated the sixth-largest web shopping site in July by MediaMetrix. For CDNow he found that revenues per customer declined in 1998 from $23.15 to $21.26. The first half of 1999, after CDNow bought a competitor N2K, brought an even more precipitous drop to $18.15 at the end of the first quarter and $14.42 in the second.

For Amazon, Von der Porten calculates a similar plunge. Revenues per customer for the fiscal quarter ended in July were $29.26, down 20 percent from a year earlier.

Looked at through this prism, Ebay also looks like a bloodbath. Faye Landes, who follows the online auction leader for Thomas Weisel Partners, estimates that revenues per user declined from $10.30 in the first quarter of 1998 to $6.80 for the second quarter of this year. Significantly, the decline resists cyclical upturns around Christmas, and has been a steady drum beat since early last year.

The sharp drop at Ebay suggests that its dazzling stock gain may be masking a major weakness. Ebay's stock has gained 56 percent this year. Ebay closed yesterday at $125.5625, up $6.125, while CDNow closed at $14.125, down 22 percent for the year and well off its $16 offering price.

Internet companies are swift to point out the gaping flaw in the formula, namely that the number of customers is cumulative, not taking into account people who shop once or twice and never come back. It is inherently unfair, they say, to divide revenues for one quarter by all-time customers. "Not every person shops every quarter. So a steady decline is exactly what you would expect to see," said Bill Curry, an exasperated Amazon spokesman.

Ebay also faults the approach. "It doesn't pass the common sense test," added Steve Westly, a vice president of Ebay. "On average, the number is going down because not all customers stay, but the customer who is staying is spending so much more that it outweighs the attrition."

While stock analysts acknowledge the equation is not perfect, they say it is justified by the companies' own business model. Online merchants have long argued that they should not be judged as conventional businesses. They justify huge current loses by saying that revenues will be recouped as customers spend more. Amazon, for example, rationalizes the deficits it has rung up lately to add an auction house and a toy store to its site by reasoning that in the future, customers who previously used the site to buy just books will add a Ricky Martin CD and Pokemon cards to their shopping baskets when they come in search of the John Grisham thriller.

"They are the ones inviting this comparison and this calculation," Von Der Porten said. "E-tailers need strong repeat business in order to generate profits from their customer bases. That's why the declining per-customer revenues call into question the viability of the business model."

Sensitive as they are to the criticism, Internet retailers have not released numbers that might make such imperfect calculations unnecessary. Amazon could disclose how many customers it has each quarter, a statistic that would provide a fairer measure of growth. Will they? "Nope," said Curry.

"We consider that proprietary information."

The New York Times, August 31, 1999
http://www.nytimes.com/library/tech/99/09/biztech/articles/01place.html

CRITICAL THINKING QUESTIONS

1. Should the stocks of Internet retailers be valued differently from the stocks of traditional retailers? Why, or why not?
2. Does the formula for measuring Internet retailers—total revenues for a quarter divided by total customer base—make sense? Why, or why not?

3. What are the strengths and weaknesses of this formula?
4. What other ways could one value Internet retailers?

STORY-SPECIFIC QUESTIONS

1. What are the two numbers that E-tailers love to trumpet (because they are always growing)?
2. What formula is offered for valuing Internet retailers? What is the gaping flaw in this formula?
3. How do Internet retailers justify huge losses?

SHORT APPLICATION ASSIGNMENTS

1. In teams or individually, answer the story-specific questions; keep your answers to 25–75 words for each question.
2. In teams of three to five persons each, or as a whole class, discuss your responses to the critical thinking questions.
3. Prepare a one-page memo report (200–250 words) to your instructor in which you summarize this article. You will find a model one-page report on the Web site (nytimes.swcollege.com).
4. Write an executive summary (200–250 words). As an administrative assistant to a busy executive, you are expected to summarize selected articles and present important points. You will find a model executive summary on the Web site.
5. Summarize this article (100–125 words) for your company's newsletter. You will find a model newsletter article on the Web site.

BUILDING RESEARCH SKILLS

1. Individually or in teams, compare two traditional retailer's Web sites versus two on-line retailers' Web sites. Sears (http://www.sears.com/) and Wal-Mart http://www.walmart.com) are examples of traditional retailers, and Amazon (http://www.amazon.com) and CDNow (http://www.cdnow.com/) are examples of online retailers. Comparisons might include the site's target customer, main areas, ease of navigation and usefulness and ease of purchase. Your instructor may ask you to submit a three- to five-page essay, post a Web page or report your results in a five-minute presentation, along with a letter of transmittal explaining your findings.
2. Individually or in teams, use traditional financial ratios such as yield percentage, EPS or PE to compare the stock of retailers such as Sears, Wal-Mart, Amazon and CDNow. Your instructor may assign you specific ratios or specific companies. Your instructor may also ask you to submit a three- to five-page proposal, post a Web page or report your results in a five-minute presentation, along with a letter of transmittal explaining your proposal.

How Boards Deal With Lazy Directors

By Sana Siwolop

Though their numbers have been under downward pressure in recent years, they are still far from an endangered species: Deadwood directors who occupy seats on corporate boards but rarely bother to attend meetings or keep abreast of company matters.

Because most companies lack any formal mechanism for regularly culling and restocking their boards, corporate governance experts say, even notoriously disengaged directors might hang on for years, routinely renominated every proxy season simply because fellow directors are loath to embarrass their own by dropping them from the proxy ballot.

Over the last decade, some companies have tried to keep their boards fresh and involved, by adopting mandatory retirement ages or imposing "term limits" of 10 or 15 years' maximum tenure. About half the companies in the Standard & Poor's 500 now have one rule or the other, according to the Investor Responsibility Research Center, a group that studies corporate governance.

While they have had some effect, though, such measures have been criticized as arbitrary and ill-aimed, removing the best directors as well as the worst.

"All too often, companies use term limits as a substitute for thorough evaluations," said Donald S. Perkins, a former chairman of Jewel Companies who has served on a number of corporate boards.

Lately the focus has shifted to another approach, familiar to many a middle manager but still new in the clubby world of the boardroom: Performance evaluations.

Few companies have yet taken the idea as far as International Multifoods in Wayzata, Minnesota. The company's three-pronged policy calls for each of the company's eight directors to confidentially evaluate the board as a whole, the other seven directors individually, and themselves; the compiled evaluations are considered by the company's nominating committee when directors' three-year terms expire. Still, the effort by International Multifoods seems to represent the future.

"We're seeing two things," said Roger Raber, chief executive of the National Association of Corporate Directors. "Companies are moving more toward board evaluations, as opposed to term limits. And more are going toward a peer review process, in which board members evaluate each other individually, instead of just evaluating the board as a whole."

Promoting a healthy level of board turnover has taken on greater urgency as more companies find themselves selecting younger directors, often turning to candidates in their 40s, corporate governance experts say. Against this background, many companies cast a critical eye on mechanical solutions like term limits.

Term limits are now used by only about 8 percent of for-profit companies, but interest in director evaluations is growing, according to a recent survey of Fortune 1000 company directors by Korn/Ferry International, an executive search firm. One in five respondents said their companies already evaluated directors individually, but 73 percent said they should.

But corporate governance experts are divided over board evaluations. Some critics say they are often conducted in ways that undermine their effectiveness.

"I see some pretty funny schemes going on at boards, where the evaluations are done as if to see who is the best-liked person in the room," said Jay Lorsch, a business professor at Harvard University who has served as a consultant to some 25 boards over the last four years. The standard of conduct applied is often "both homogenous and superficial," he said, adding that he thinks better results are achieved by having an outside consultant write the evaluations after interviewing directors.

Other experts say that's fine in theory but problematic in practice. "The problem with the outsider model is that it's very hard to find that outsider whom the entire board trusts," said Phil Lochner, a former Securities and Exchange Commissioner who now sits on a number of corporate boards.

Lochner prefers term limits; he thinks evaluating individual directors properly is difficult and can be unfair if the company has no written performance standards for them, as most do not.

Still, some companies are forging ahead. At International Multifoods, Gary Costley, the chief executive, acknowledged that getting peer review started at his company has been "tricky" because, he said, directors tend to have thin skins and large, fragile egos.

The board came around to the idea after Costley first submitted to formal evaluation himself, and showed he was prepared to take criticism. "I don't think you can have an effective board evaluation process unless you first have an effective CEO evaluation process," he said.

Even so, some Multifoods directors have resigned, Costley said. And, he added, a few prospects have shied away from joining the board because of the evaluation system.

The resistance doesn't surprise some experts, who think evaluations will be a short-lived boardroom fad. "People feel very funny about offending the people they work with," said Charles Elson, a law professor at Stetson University in St. Petersburg, Florida. An oil and gas company on whose board he sits, Nuevo Energy in Houston, recently considered and rejected an evaluation system. "We thought term limits would be more effective over all," he said.

Richard H. Koppes, a lawyer at Jones, Day, Reavis & Pogue in Sacramento, California, who specializes in governance issues, wonders whether even perfectly frank evaluations can achieve much. Many directors will remain unwilling or unable to shape up, he said, and boards will probably opt to tough out their tenure rather than confront them.

An article by Koppes in Corporate Governance Advisor, a professional journal, proposes an alternative for keeping boards fresh: setting a maximum average tenure and replacing long-tenured directors only when the board as a whole exceeds the maximum.

Under his plan, boards with a healthy mix of new and old directors would not lose valuable members to an arbitrary term limit, but stale boards would get an objective signal to bring in new blood.

So far, governance experts have given Koppes high marks for trying to make term limits less arbitrary. But many wonder whether there might not be a simpler way for companies to freshen their boards.

"Nominating committees should do their job right and elect people for two or three years and then reassess them," Lorsch said. "But I suspect that only 15 to 20 percent of companies do this."

The New York Times, October 17, 1999
http://www.nytimes.com/library/financial/sunday/101799invest-boards.html

CRITICAL THINKING QUESTIONS

1. Why do some companies lack any formal mechanism for regularly culling and re-stocking their board of directors?
2. What policies and procedures would you suggest in order to keep directors fresh and involved?
3. What are the advantages and disadvantages of term limits for directors?
4. What are the advantages and disadvantages of age limits for directors?
5. What are the advantages and disadvantages of evaluating directors?

STORY-SPECIFIC QUESTIONS

1. According to the Investor Responsibility Research Center, about one-half of the S&P 500 corporations have adopted what two methods in order to keep their boards fresh and involved?
2. Roger Raber, chief executive of the National Association of Corporate Directors, sees what two trends?
3. What formula does Richard H. Koppes propose as an alternative for keeping boards fresh?

SHORT APPLICATION ASSIGNMENTS

1. In teams or individually, answer the story-specific questions; keep your answers to 25–75 words for each question.

2. In teams of three to five persons each, or as a whole class, discuss your responses to the critical thinking questions.
3. Prepare a one-page memo report (200–250 words) to your instructor in which you summarize this article. You will find a model one-page report on the Web site (nytimes.swcollege.com).
4. Write an executive summary (200–250 words). As an administrative assistant to a busy executive, you are expected to summarize selected articles and present important points. You will find a model executive summary on the Web site.
5. Summarize this article (100–125 words) for your company's newsletter. You will find a model newsletter article on the Web site.
6. Individually or in teams, research the board of directors of a publicly traded corporation. Topics might include the board's number of members, shares owned, average tenure, average age and other demographic variables. Your instructor may ask you to present your findings in an oral report or submit a 150- to 200-word summary.

BUILDING RESEARCH SKILLS

1. Individually or in teams, compare the Web sites of four companies in the Dow Jones industrial average. What information about its board of directors does each site contain? Was this information easy to find? Your instructor may ask you to submit a three- to five-page essay, post a Web page or report your results in a five-minute presentation, along with a letter of transmittal explaining your findings.
2. Using at least three other references (e.g., books, research-journal articles, newspaper or magazine stories or credible Web sites), write an 800- to 1,000-word essay that addresses two of the critical thinking questions offered earlier. Assume that your essay will be used as an internal reference for a financial institution's corporate governance guidelines.
3. Using at least three other references (e.g., books, research-journal articles, newspaper or magazine stories or credible Web sites), post an 800- to 1,000-word Web page that addresses at least two of the earlier critical thinking questions. Assume that your page will be posted in the investment section of a corporate intranet.

Financial Institutions and Monetary Policy

PREVIEW

Monetary theorists, politicians and lobbyists for industries such as banking, insurance and securities are among the experts attempting to influence monetary policy. Most agree that the Federal Reserve or legislation can influence finance both globally and in the United States, but the experts disagree on how that influence works and on the appropriate legislation or Federal Reserve policy.

Politicians and lobbyists, however, were of the same mind on opening up the U.S. financial system. In "Agreement Reached on Overhaul of U.S. Financial System," Stephen Labaton explains this recent accord. The legislation will repeal Depression-era laws that keep the banking, securities and insurance industries from expanding into one another's businesses.

While experts agreed on overhauling the U.S. financial system, they most likely disagree on the Federal Reserve's role, influence and appropriate policy. As Sylvia Nasar explores in "Inflation Just Doesn't Add Up," transitory factors, structural changes, policy changes, energy prices, globalization, deregulation, the computer revolution and Fed Chairman Alan Greenspan are among the interrelated parts that confound expert advice on inflation.

Although most economies take inflation for granted, deflation also exists. In what may seem like a consumer's paradise, prices continue to fall. But as Mark Landler reports in "Amid Unrest, Chinese Face an Ugly Reality: Deflation," leaders in China's capital of Beijing face a formidable problem to correct. Chinese consumers are so worried about their future that they have stopped buying.

Agreement Reached on Overhaul of U.S. Financial System

By Stephen Labaton

WASHINGTON—The Clinton Administration and top Republican law-makers reached an agreement early Friday to overhaul the financial system, re-pealing Depression-era laws that have restricted the banking, securities and insurance industries from expanding into one another's businesses.

The deal was announced about 2 A.M. after a compromise was reached over the measure's effect on lending rules for the disadvantaged, the source of months of partisan bickering between the White House and Senator Phil Gramm, the Texas Republican who heads the banking committee.

It concludes decades of attempts to rewrite banking laws to catch up with a marketplace that has already experienced broad consolidations and the rise of financial conglomerates offering bank and brokerage accounts as well as insurance.

While these conglomerates have found ways around the old rules, those rules had made it expensive and at times impossible to expand into new lines of financial services.

For instance, the nation's largest financial services company, Citigroup, would have been forced to sell some of its insurance operations as part of the $72 billion merger last year between Citibank and Travelers Group without either the legislation or a waiver from regulators.

With such situations in mind, the banking, insurance and securities industries spent more than $300 million in 1997 and 1998 alone on a combination of donations to political candidates, soft money contributions to political parties and lobbying.

The legislation will more easily enable financial companies to offer corporate clients a full range of services, from traditional loans to investment banking services, like public stock offerings. And for consumers, it paves the way for financial supermarkets, which will be able to offer one-stop shopping for an array of services, all under one roof. The measure is also expected to clear a path for a new and bigger wave of corporate deal-making as more companies consolidate.

White House officials withheld final approval of the agreement until aides could see the measure's language. But the officials indicated Friday night that, with broad support from Democrats in Congress, the measure was all but certain to be signed by President Clinton. As such, it will be one of the most significant pieces of legislation to be written by the White House and the 106th Congress, which began its term considering whether to remove Clinton and has had a bitter relationship ever since.

"When this potentially historic agreement is finalized," Clinton said in a statement, "it will strengthen the economy and help consumers, communities and businesses across America."

Treasury Secretary Lawrence H. Summers said in an interview, "At the end of the twentieth century, we will at last be replacing an archaic set of restrictions with a legislative foundation for a twenty-first-century financial system." The measure, he added, "would provide significant benefits to the national economy."

Senator Gramm said the measure "is the most important banking legislation in 60 years."

Gramm's counterpart in the House, Representative James A. Leach of Iowa, said that he expected a final bill to be brought to the House and Senate floors later this month.

While the measure is likely to enjoy broad bipartisan support, it has also been criticized. Some lawmakers and privacy groups say the legislation does not adequately protect consumers and will allow financial companies to share and sell private information about customer accounts. Other critics worry about the further consolidation of the financial services industry.

The legislation repeals the Glass-Steagall Act, or, as it is formally known, the Banking Act of 1933, which broke up the powerful House of Morgan and divided Wall Street between investment banks and commercial banks. It also makes significant changes to the Bank Holding Company Act of 1956, which had restricted what banks could do in the insurance business.

The Glass-Steagall Act was enacted after the stock market crash of 1929 and the ensuing banking crisis and Great Depression. On the day it was signed, along with the National Industrial Recovery Act and other measures, President Franklin D. Roosevelt called the package "the most important and far-reaching legislation ever enacted by the American Congress."

The idea behind Glass-Steagall, named for the two lawmakers who wrote it, was that confidence in America's financial house could best be restored if bankers and brokers stayed in separate rooms. Such a separation, it was thought, achieved two purposes.

First, it would reduce the potential conflicts of interest between investment banking and commercial banking that were thought to have contributed to the speculative frenzy in the stock markets. Under the 1933 Banking Act, commercial banks could receive no more than 10 percent of their income from the securities markets, a limit so restrictive that most simply abandoned business on Wall Street.

Second, it would provide a safe harbor for the money of ordinary Americans by enabling them to put their money in accounts that were protected by deposit insurance and insulated from more speculative investments like stocks. (The 1933 act also established the Federal Deposit Insurance Corporation, which now insures bank deposits up to $100,000.)

Over time, Federal judges and regulators chipped away at the Glass-Steagall Act and other restrictions on cross-ownership of banks, insurance companies and securities firms, enabling, for instance, Citibank to merge with Travelers last year to form Citigroup, the world's largest financial services company. But large hurdles remained that have discouraged the expansion by banks into new businesses.

The breakthrough in Friday's legislation came in a backroom meeting at the Capitol soon after midnight, when a group of moderate Senate Democrats— led by Christopher Dodd of Connecticut and Charles E. Schumer of New York—forced a compromise between Gramm and the White House over the legislation's effect on the Community Reinvestment Act, a 1977 anti-discrimination law intended to encourage lending to minorities and others historically denied access to credit.

Dodd, whose state is home to the nation's largest insurance companies, and Schumer, with strong ties to Wall Street, have long sought legislation to repeal the Glass-Steagall Act. Both men said in interviews Friday that they moved to strike a compromise after it became apparent that the legislation might be killed, as it was last year by Gramm, over the debate about the Community Reinvestment Act.

Gramm had maintained that he did not want anything in the bill that would expand the application of the Community Reinvestment Act because it was, he said, unnecessarily burdensome to banks. He had sought a provision that would exempt thousands of smaller banks from the law. He also wanted a provision that would expose what he has described as the "extortion" committed by community groups against banks by requiring the groups to disclose any special financial deals the groups extract from the banks.

But the White House found that provision unacceptable and had its own ideas about community lending. It wanted the legislation to prevent any bank with an unsatisfactory record of making loans to the disadvantaged from expanding into new areas, like insurance or securities.

The White House had insisted that the President would veto any legislation that would scale back minority-lending requirements. Four days of intense negotiations between Summers, Gene Sperling, the President's top economic policy adviser, and Gramm, while moving the two sides closer, failed to resolve the differences.

Such was the state of play Thursday evening when Gramm decided to force the issue by having the House-Senate conference committee vote on his proposed compromise, which the White House had already rejected for failing to block banks with bad lending records from expanding to new businesses.

When Gramm's measure was defeated by one vote, it quickly became clear that there would be no law unless Gramm could get some Democrats to break from the White House.

But Administration officials had spent all day making sure that the Democrats remained solidly against the measure until their concerns about the Community Reinvestment Act could be worked out.

After receiving calls from executives of some of the nation's leading financial companies, Dodd and Schumer began trying to work out a compromise. An agreement was quickly reached on the issue of banks and expanded powers—no institution would be allowed to move into any new lines of business without a satisfactory lending record.

The lawmakers bogged down on Gramm's insistence that all community organizations disclose to the regulators what benefits they get from banks. Some Democrats expressed the fear that Gramm's proposal would require the Boy Scouts to file reports with the regulators.

Ultimately, the following provisions were drawn up and both the White House and Gramm said they could accept them:

- Banks will not be able to move into new lines of business unless they have satisfactory lending records.
- Community groups will have to make disclosures to regulators about certain kinds of financial deals with banks that they have pressed to make loans under the Community Reinvestment Act.
- Wholesale financial institutions, a new kind of business that takes large, uninsured bank deposits, cannot be affiliated with commercial banks.
- Small banks with satisfactory or excellent track records of lending to the underserved would be reviewed less frequently under the Community Reinvestment Act. As a practical matter smaller banks are reviewed about every three years. The deal struck today allows all rural banks and banks with less than $250 million in assets to undergo examination once every five years if their last exam resulted in an "outstanding" grade and every four years if they last scored "satisfactory."

For more than 20 years, Congress has tried unsuccessfully to rewrite the nation's financial services laws and repeal Glass-Steagall, particularly as many other industrial nations had no similar restrictions on their banks. But until recently, the three main industries affected by the legislation—banks, securities companies and insurers—had competing interests and were able to lobby any legislation to a standstill.

That all changed in recent years as the lines between the industries began to blur and it became more broadly acknowledged that a deregulation of financial services could be beneficial to insurers, bankers and securities firms alike. Once the three industries rallied around the legislation, they became a formidable political force, raising millions of dollars for lawmakers and pressing both Republican leaders in Congress and the White House for new legislation.

The New York Times, October 23, 1999
http://www.nytimes.com/library/financial/102399banks-congress.html

CRITICAL THINKING QUESTIONS

1. How will the recently passed legislation benefit or harm consumers?
2. Should banks be allowed to add other services such as insurance or investing in the stock market? Why, or why not?
3. Do you support this legislation? Why, or why not?
4. What are the advantages and disadvantages of this legislation for the banking industry? For the insurance industry? For the securities industry?

STORY-SPECIFIC QUESTIONS

1. The recently passed legislation repeals many laws from what era? What did these prior laws restrict?
2. How much money did banking, insurance and securities industries spend in 1997 and 1998 on donations to political candidates, soft money contributions to political parties and lobbying?
3. Critics are raising what issues concerning this legislation?
4. What were the two main ideas behind the Glass-Steagall Act, or, as it is formally known, the Banking Act of 1933?

SHORT APPLICATION ASSIGNMENTS

1. In teams or individually, answer the story-specific questions; keep your answers to 25–75 words for each question.
2. In teams of three to five persons each, or as a whole class, discuss your responses to the critical thinking questions.
3. Prepare a one-page memo report (200–250 words) to your instructor in which you summarize this article. You will find a model one-page report on the Web site (nytimes.swcollege.com).
4. Write an executive summary (200–250 words). As an administrative assistant to a busy executive, you are expected to summarize selected articles and present important points. You will find a model executive summary on the Web site.
5. Summarize this article (100–125 words) for your company's newsletter. You will find a model newsletter article on the Web site.
6. Individually or in teams, research the recent services offered by a major bank, insurance or securities company. What services have they added? What mergers or alliances have they made? Your instructor may ask you to present your findings in an oral report or submit a 150- to 200-word summary.

BUILDING RESEARCH SKILLS

1. Individually or in teams, research the merger of Citibank and The Travelers Group. Be sure to include the Citigroup Web site (http://www.citigroup.com) and Leslie Wayne's story, "Financial Industry Awaits Biggest Transformation Since Depression (http://www.nytimes.com/library/financial/070299banking-deregulation.html)" as

part of your research. Your instructor may ask you to submit a three- to five-page essay, post a Web page or report your results in a five-minute presentation, along with a letter of transmittal explaining your findings.

2. Using at least three other references (e.g., books, research-journal articles, newspaper or magazine stories or credible Web sites), write an 800- to 1,000-word essay that addresses two of the critical thinking questions offered earlier. Assume that your essay will be used as an internal reference for a financial institution's services department.

3. Using at least three other references (e.g., books, research-journal articles, newspaper or magazine stories or credible Web sites), post an 800- to 1,000-word Web page that addresses at least two of the earlier critical thinking questions. Assume that your page will be posted in the services section of a financial institutions corporate intranet.

Inflation Just Doesn't Add Up

By Sylvia Nasar

Barely a year after a worldwide deflation scare—when markets and currencies were crashing, banks and businesses in Asia, Russia and Latin America were failing, and prices of oil and raw materials were plunging—inflation is back on peoples' minds.

On the face of it, fretting about inflation when every major price gauge in the United States is rising just 2 percent or so a year seems a little like Uma Thurman obsessing over her weight. But what concerns Alan Greenspan, the Federal Reserve chairman, and Wall Street investors is the nagging suspicion that the stellar inflation record of the last two years was mostly the product of a few lucky, highly transitory breaks—and therefore won't last. That suspicion is likely to propel the Fed's policy-making committee toward another interest-rate increase when it meets on Tuesday.

Admittedly, the budding recovery in Asia and Europe has already blunted some of the forces that have helped push U.S. inflation down from 4 percent to 2 percent a year since 1997. Energy prices—indeed, most commodity prices other than farm products—are already rebounding sharply after collapsing last year. And the high-flying dollar, which helped to make imports cheaper, has recently weakened against the euro and the yen as global investors have begun to shift some of their mutual fund money away from the United States to foreign markets.

Sounds dire, right? Actually, there are solid reasons for thinking that a return to the bad old days, when upwardly spiraling prices seemed as inevitable as the sunrise, is highly unlikely. For one thing, some of those "transitory" factors are likely to persist for quite a while longer. For another, popular expectations about inflation—low inflation, this time—readily become self-fulfilling prophecies. And a host of structural and policy changes over the last couple of decades have made the U.S. economy less inherently prone to inflation.

Even skeptics now say that the low inflation of the 1990s is not just a fluke, but rather a return to a norm that prevailed for a quarter-century, beginning in the late 1940s—years when 4 percent inflation seemed scandalously high. As Alan S. Blinder, an economist at Princeton University and former vice chairman of the Federal Reserve, said recently, "To a substantial extent, we're back to the '50s."

Jeffrey Frankel of Harvard University, until recently a member of the President's Council of Economic Advisers, said of mainstream economists: "A lot of us were real stick-in-the-muds. We said: 'No, no, no. Here are the equations.' But other people who knew less about equations had the sense to realize that things are a bit different."

For starters, not all the good luck is evaporating. True, energy prices have jumped 24 percent since the beginning of the year. But energy wasn't a big factor in inflation's decline—the economy uses a lot less energy than it did in, say, 1973—and this year's price increase isn't anything like the surges in 1973 or 1990. Most of the impact has already filtered through to consumer prices for gasoline, electricity, heating oil and air fares, adding at most a few tenths of a percentage point to the inflation rate.

The dollar's recent dip and the ballooning trade deficit have some economists, notably Paul Krugman of the Massachusetts Institute of Technology, warning of the possibility of a currency crisis. If the dollar were to take a big dive, that would indeed threaten to push inflation up sharply. But it would also provoke a sharp reaction from the Fed. And the dollar is still slightly stronger on a trade-weighted basis (that is, against a basket of currencies of America's trading partners) than it was at the start of the year.

More to the point, import prices, by far the biggest recent drag on inflation, are apt to remain under downward pressure. Their decline, it turns out, was due less to the strong dollar than to vast excess productive capacity in Asia, Latin America and elsewhere—an excess that will not be mopped up soon, given the gradual pace of world recovery. "It's not just the dollar, but economic incentives to increase production abroad," said Robert J. Gordon, an economist at Northwestern University.

Domestically, health care costs have stopped skyrocketing and show few signs of resuming that course, despite increases over the last year in the fees that health maintenance organizations charge employers. Though the latest readings show consumer prices for medical care rising a bit faster than a year ago, few experts expect the pace to accelerate to twice the overall inflation rate, as it did in the early 1990s.

In any case, even temporary lulls in inflation can have long-term effects, by changing expectations. Americans who believed two decades ago that inflation would always rise are now expecting it to remain low. According to the monthly University of Michigan survey of consumer expectations, ordinary Americans expect the inflation rate a year from now to be under 3 percent. (The Federal Reserve forecasts 2.5 percent or less.) "You get this extra impact," Gordon said. "The biggest factor holding down inflation in the next couple of years is the lower inflation of the past couple."

But perhaps the strongest reasons for optimism are sweeping changes in the economy that have been in the works for years.

Back in the bad old 1970s, temporary supply shocks tended to produce higher inflation automatically. Since then, some long-term trends—globalization, deregulation, the computer revolution—have made the economy less susceptible to bottlenecks and wage-price spirals. "One story is that we are permanently able to run the economy hotter and labor markets tighter," Krugman said, "because we have a more flexible labor market, and monopoly and union power have been curbed by international competition."

Consider deregulation, which began during the Carter administration and has since radically transformed broad swaths of the sprawling service sector, including airlines, energy, banking, railroads, telecommunications and, most recently, electricity. More competition helps rein in inflation directly, and a new wealth of alternatives keeps strikes or other disruptions from creating bottlenecks. (Remember what life was like before faxes, cell phones and e-mail?) "They all kind of connect the economy together," Frankel said.

Then there's the computer revolution. Information technology helps companies do everything they do—notably, managing inventory—more flexibly and efficiently. But innovation is also driving down computer prices, and rapidly enough to take half a percentage point off the overall inflation rate, according to Gordon.

More prosaic changes in the way the American labor market works may be as important as globalization. Alan B. Krueger of Princeton University and Lawrence F. Katz of Harvard recently published a study suggesting that a host of small, incremental changes—including the decline of unions, the growing role of temporary-help firms, even welfare reform—have made the labor market more efficient. That may be why an unemployment rate below the prevailing average of the 1950s and 1960s has yet to set off bidding wars among employers.

And though the labor market may be tight, American business is still operating with a lot of spare capacity, the product of an investment boom spurred by lower interest rates and a rush to embrace technology. Utilization rates remain relatively low even after eight years of economic expansion—one reason that companies find it hard to raise prices. "That could explain why inflation is lower than you'd think just looking at unemployment," Frankel said.

That investment boom has had another powerful anti-inflation effect. Productivity has been growing at around 2 percent a year, double the rate that prevailed in the 1970s and 1980s. Greater efficiency, in turn, has made it possible for employers to increase compensation at a higher pace than the inflation rate without adding much to their costs. "We've had an acceleration of productivity growth, and it takes a while before people build that expectation into wages," Krugman said.

Of course, even the most open, flexible, productive economy can suffer inflation. Inflation, as Milton Friedman, the Nobel Prize-winning economist, has said, is ultimately a monetary phenomenon, and is therefore determined by policy makers in Washington, most notably the Fed. Recall how the low-inflation post-war era ended: tax cuts and guns-and-butter spending under Presidents Kennedy and Johnson and an accommodating central bank let the inflation genie out of the bottle even before the Organization of Petroleum Exporting Countries quadrupled oil prices in 1973.

Putting the genie back in the bottle cost the nation a couple of nasty recessions and years of high unemployment and lost output. Today, the memory of the high human and political costs of wringing inflation out of the system helps keep inflation at bay, much as memories of the Great Depression have kept deflation at bay. Three times in 10 years, Alan Greenspan has struck pre-emptively with interest-rate increases to ward off any acceleration before it could even begin, in 1989, 1994 and now—strikes that so far, at least, seem to have served the economy well.

The New York Times, August 22, 1999
http://www.nytimes.com/library/financial/fed/082299econ-inflation.html

CRITICAL THINKING QUESTIONS

1. What is the appropriate inflation rate for a healthy U.S. economy? Explain.
2. How, and to what extent, can the Federal Reserve control the U.S. economy? The world economy?
3. Does the Federal Reserve yield too much power? Why, or why not?
4. How do currency exchange rates influence inflation?
5. Is a little bit of inflation a good thing? Why, or why not?
6. Can popular expectations about inflation, such as low inflation, readily become self-fulfilling prophecies? Why, or why not?

STORY-SPECIFIC QUESTIONS

1. What are three solid reasons for thinking that a return to the bad old days, when upwardly spiraling prices seemed as inevitable as the sunrise, is highly unlikely?
2. Why wasn't energy a big factor in inflation's decline?
3. Who is the chairman of the Federal Reserve?
4. What three long-term trends have made the economy less susceptible to bottlenecks and wage-price spirals?

SHORT APPLICATION ASSIGNMENTS

1. In teams or individually, answer the story-specific questions; keep your answers to 25–75 words for each question.
2. In teams of three to five persons each, or as a whole class, discuss your responses to the critical thinking questions.
3. Prepare a one-page memo report (200–250 words) to your instructor in which you summarize this article. You will find a model one-page report on the Web site (nytimes.swcollege.com).
4. Write an executive summary (200–250 words). As an administrative assistant to a busy executive, you are expected to summarize selected articles and present impor-tant points. You will find a model executive summary on the Web site.
5. Summarize this article (100–125 words) for your company's newsletter. You will find a model newsletter article on the Web site.

BUILDING RESEARCH SKILLS

1. Individually or in teams, research the last three Federal Reserve meetings. A good starting point for your research is *The New York Times on the Web*'s special section on the Federal Reserve (http://www.nytimes.com/library/financial/fed/index-fed.html). What action did the Fed take? What did the finance community think of the Fed's action? Your instructor may ask you to submit a three- to five-page essay, post a Web page or report your results in a five-minute presentation, along with a letter of transmittal explaining your findings.

2. Individually or in teams, compare the U.S. inflation rate to that of three other countries. What are the forecasts for each country? Why are their inflation rates different? How does each country attempt to control their respective inflation rates? Your instructor may ask you to submit a three- to five-page essay, post a Web page or report your results in a five-minute presentation, along with a letter of transmittal explaining your findings.

3. Using at least three other references (e.g., books, research-journal articles, newspaper or magazine stories or credible Web sites), write an 800- to 1,000-word essay that addresses two of the critical thinking questions offered earlier. Assume that your essay will be used as an internal reference for a financial institution's investment guidelines.

4. Using at least three other references (e.g., books, research-journal articles, newspaper or magazine stories or credible Web sites), post an 800- to 1,000-word Web page that addresses at least two of the earlier critical thinking questions. Assume that your page will be posted in the investment section of a corporate intranet.

Amid Unrest, Chinese Face an Ugly Reality: Deflation

By Mark Landler

BEIJING—China's top leaders fled the stifling heat of Beijing last week for their annual retreat at a seaside resort, leaving behind a city swirling with propaganda about the crackdown on a spiritual movement known as Falun Gong.

But while the Communist Party has mounted a relentless media assault on the group, which it outlawed on Thursday, economics rather than politics are likely to occupy the leaders as they gather in the tranquil resort of Beidaihe. Specifically, analysts here say they will have to confront China's economy, which is sputtering, and a reform effort that is in danger of stalling.

"The attack on Falun Gong comes at a time when they have so much more to worry about," a party functionary in Beijing said. "We should be concerned about developing the economy. There's a risk that this will distract everyone's attention."

In particular, Beijing must figure out how to rebuild the confidence of battered Chinese consumers. For 21 consecutive months, consumer prices in China have fallen. That is because, in economic terms, China is in a deflationary spiral, which means that consumers who are worried about their futures have stopped buying things.

The deflation has been aggravated by a huge glut in production capacity. Too many factories are making too many goods, a lot of which do not appeal to China's jaded shoppers.

"It's a very worrying set of circumstances," said T. L. Tsim, an independent consultant on Chinese politics and economics in Hong Kong. "Once deflation takes hold, it is very hard to shake off."

Tsim said the downward spiral in prices had slowed China's once-torrid economic growth and could hobble it further. It could also derail the radical reforms of China's bloated state-owned industries that Prime Minister Zhu Rongji announced with much fanfare in the spring of 1998.

Although China said its economy grew 7.8 percent last year, economists say the real figure was closer to 4 percent. Even the official estimates confirm that growth has slowed each year since 1996.

Maintaining robust growth is crucial in China because with a population of 1.3 billion that expands at 1 percent a year, the country must add at least 7.5 million jobs a year just to absorb the people entering the labor force. And that does nothing to alleviate the existing unemployment rate, which economists estimate at 10 percent in urban areas and 30 percent in the hinterland.

Zhu's reform of state industries will necessitate closing down hundreds of inefficient state-owned companies, which could throw millions of workers on the streets. The prospect of these layoffs—in addition to a loss of benefits and subsidies as Beijing dismantles its Communist welfare state—has left many Chinese people deeply insecure about their future.

"People used to have very little money in their pockets, but most things were allocated by the government," said Ding Junfa, deputy director of the state Administration for Domestic Trade. "Now people's expectations are changing. They are putting money aside."

The flowering of spiritual movements in such an atmosphere is not surprising. The popular discontent that flows from a torpid economy supplies the kindling for groups like Falun Gong, whose followers draw solace from a blend of Buddhism, Taoism and breathing exercises.

The government apparently reacted so strongly to the unexpected emergence of Falun Gong in April because it recognized the group's success as a symptom of a deeper social and economic malaise.

There are other reasons Chinese people flock to these sects, of course—not the least that after two decades of a more open society, the Communist Party's values no longer seem particularly relevant to many Chinese. But at least some analysts said that people's fear of economic upheaval appears to be one driving motivation for turning to such groups now.

"Under Mao Tse-tung, people felt everything was handed to them. There was no competition," said Dai Qing, a commentator in Beijing. "Since the Deng Xiaoping era, there has been more and more competition. People feel they have no control over their future, especially older people."

Ms. Dai said one reason Falun Gong thrives is that it promises to improve the health of practitioners by harnessing traditional Chinese breathing and meditation exercises, known as qigong. Such remedies may provide some comfort at a time when the state no longer provides free health care.

"Nowadays people have to pay 70, 80, 90 percent of their medical expenses," Ms. Dai said. "But many people find it impossible to pay such large costs, so they turn to other ways of staying fit and healing themselves. That's why Falun Gong and other types of qigong have so many adherents."

In addition to those seeking spiritual nourishment, people are expressing their insecurities in a more tangible way: They are stashing their paychecks in the bank. The savings rate in China is roughly 42 percent of household income, one of the highest in the world. And it is rising as consumer spending weakens.

By Western standards, consumer spending in China still looks fine. For a rapidly-developing country, though, the trend is disturbing. Officials said the growth in consumer spending had tapered off steadily in recent years, from 10.2 percent in 1997 to 6.8 percent in 1998 and 6.4 percent in the first half of this year.

Evidence of the new parsimony—and abundant overconstruction of new stores—abounds at the glittering shopping malls that line Beijing's Changan Avenue. At the Henderson Center, a multilevel temple to consumerism that opened last year, a mere handful of shoppers drifted past boutiques that trumpeted clearance sales the other day.

Wang Taochun hurried past the stores. "I'm like everyone else," said Wang, a 24-year-old clerk at a computer firm. "How much I spend depends on how much I earn. Right now, I'm not earning enough."

A similar scene unfolded at a nearby department store. Although color television sets were selling at deep discounts, a sales clerk confided that she would be lucky to sell one a day. Last year, she said, she was selling eight a day. Next to the showroom, boxes of new sets were stacked up three deep.

A 65-year-old retired doctor who would give only his surname, Zhou, peered at a set that was selling at a 25 percent discount. "I think the price is going to go down even further," he said, "so I'm going to wait a while before I buy anything."

Zhou says he is more likely than younger consumers to replace his television set because he is living on a reliable pension. Young people, he says, have to weigh major purchases carefully because neither their jobs nor their pensions are secure.

The oversupply of television sets in China has set off such a price war that eight manufacturers of television tubes recently agreed to suspend operations for two months to reduce their stockpiles.

"There was a vicious cycle of lower and lower prices and less and less in profits," said a sales manager at one of the manufacturers. "We hope this will have some effect, but it's going to take a long time to solve the basic problems."

The most intractable problem is that there are simply too many factories churning out everything from refrigerators to air conditioners to cars. Camera factories, for example, are operating at less than 20 percent of capacity, according to government statistics. Even companies that produce China's once-ubiquitous mode of transportation, the bicycle, are running at no more than half their capacity.

The glut of capacity is a result of the foreign money that poured into China in the mid-1990s, leading the economy to grow at a furious pace. Many of those dollars flowed into hapless ventures or speculative schemes that are now losing money. One of China's largest state-owned companies, Guangdong International Trust and Investment Co., declared bankruptcy in October, leaving dozens of foreign banks holding bad loans.

Some economists contend there is little the government can do to ease price deflation, since it is caused as much by the surfeit of supply as by the lack of demand.

Until now, Beijing has focused on reviving consumer demand. It has plowed billions of dollars into vast infrastructure projects, cut interest rates, announced plans to raise salaries of civil servants by 30 percent and introduced tax credits to promote exports.

In recent months, the efforts have taken on an air of desperation. The state is encouraging more families to send their children to private colleges so that the parents will dig into their pockets for tuition. And last month, it began singing the virtues of investing in the stock market.

The campaign, promoted in official publications, prompted a flood of purchases, which drove up China's two main stock exchanges, Shanghai and Shenzhen. The shares promptly plummeted after Taiwan and China began a bitter row over defiant remarks by Taiwan's president, Lee Teng-hui.

"Talking up the market was extremely risky," said Shawn Xu, chief of research at China International Capital Corp. "Investors may hold the government responsible if the market crashes."

Like other economists, Xu said China could stimulate consumer demand only by supporting its private sector. To do that, he said, the government must overhaul its debt-ridden state banks and open its capital markets, which are still off limits to many private entrepreneurs.

He acknowledges that this is no easy task. Two decades after Deng Xiaoping began transforming China from a planned economy to a market economy, the country is entering the most painful and perilous chapter of its transformation.

"Zhu Rongji is dealing with the things that Deng Xiaoping didn't want to deal with," said Andy Xie, an economist at Morgan Stanley, Dean Witter in Hong Kong. "That's why this is so difficult."

The New York Times, July 24, 1999
http://www.nytimes.com/library/world/asia/072599china-economy.html

CRITICAL THINKING QUESTIONS

1. What is the appropriate inflation rate for a healthy Chinese economy? Explain.
2. How, and to what extent, can China control its economy? The world economy?
3. Is a little bit of deflation a good thing? Why, or why not?
4. How do currency exchange rates influence deflation?
5. What are the advantages and disadvantages of a planned economy? Of a market economy?

STORY-SPECIFIC QUESTIONS

1. How are some Chinese consumers reacting to China's deflationary spiral?
2. What production factor has aggravated China's deflation?
3. What is China's estimated unemployment rate?
4. What have Chinese officials said concerning the trends in their country's consumer spending?
5. How has Beijing focused on reviving consumer demand?

SHORT APPLICATION ASSIGNMENTS

1. In teams or individually, answer the story-specific questions; keep your answers to 25–75 words for each question.
2. In teams of three to five persons each, or as a whole class, discuss your responses to the critical thinking questions.
3. Prepare a one-page memo report (200–250 words) to your instructor in which you summarize this article. You will find a model one-page report on the Web site (nytimes.swcollege.com)
4. Write an executive summary (200–250 words). As an administrative assistant to a busy executive, you are expected to summarize selected articles and present important points. You will find a model executive summary on the Web site.
5. Summarize this article (100–125 words) for your company's newsletter. You will find a model newsletter article on the Web site.
6. Individually or in teams, research the Chinese financial markets today. What is their inflation rate? Unemployment rate? What actions is the government taking to influence the Chinese economy? Two good starting points for your research are the Bureau of East Asian and Pacific Affairs of the U.S. Department of State (http://www.state.gov/www/current/debate/china.html) and China.com (http://english.china.com). Your instructor may ask you to present your findings in an oral report or submit a 150- to 200-word summary.

BUILDING RESEARCH SKILLS

1. Individually or in teams, research the Chinese financial markets and institutions. What are the appropriate governmental agencies? What actions can these agencies take today? Two good starting points for your research are the Bureau of East Asian and Pacific Affairs of the U.S. Department of State (http://www.state.gov/www/current/debate/china.html) and China.com (http://english.china.com). Your instructor may ask you to submit a three- to five-page essay, post a Web page or report your results in a five-minute presentation, along with a letter of transmittal explaining your findings.
2. Individually or in teams, compare the Chinese inflation rate to that of three other countries. What are the forecasts for each country? Why are their inflation rates different? How does each country attempt to control their respective inflation rates? Your instructor may ask you to submit a three- to five-page essay, post a Web page or report your results in a five-minute presentation, along with a letter of transmittal explaining your findings.
3. Using at least three other references (e.g., books, research-journal articles, newspaper or magazine stories or credible Web sites), write an 800- to 1,000-word essay that addresses two of the critical thinking questions offered earlier. Assume that your essay will be used as an internal reference for a financial institution's investment guidelines.
4. Using at least three other references (e.g., books, research-journal articles, newspaper or magazine stories or credible Web sites), post an 800- to 1,000-word Web page that addresses at least two of the earlier critical thinking questions. Assume that your page will be posted in the investment section of a corporate intranet.

CHAPTER 3

Technology's Impact on Finance

PREVIEW

Computers and the Internet add a technological twist to plans by U.S. policy makers for the eventual convergence of the country's banking, insurance and security industries. Financial firms ponder if, and how, they should add products and services such as online banking, online stock trading, day trading, and shopping on the Web. And as online transactions grow, keeping this financial information secure—encrypting it—becomes increasingly important.

Traditional brokerage firms are migrating to the Internet, spurred on by technology and competition from electronic upstarts such as E*Trade. In "Morgan Stanley to Offer Online Trading to All Its Customers," Joseph Kahn and Patrick McGeehan explain how the brokerage firm will overhaul its business to offer clients the opportunity to buy and sell stocks online at discount prices.

Traditional brokers also are investigating a recent Internet financial phenomenon—day trading. As David Barboza reports in "Why Big Firms Are Courting the Day Traders," leading investment and securities firms are interested in forming alliances with or outright acquiring day-trading companies, as well as adopting their software.

Encryption software is another technology that the financial industry is warily embracing. And as Peter Wayner shows in "Attacks on Encryption Code Raise Questions About Computer Vulnerability," a great way to test this software is by trying to crack it.

Source: Christine M. Thompson/CyberTimes

Morgan Stanley to Offer Online Trading to All Its Customers

By Joseph Kahn and Patrick McGeehan

In old-line Wall Street's latest entry into the Internet stock-trading bazaar, Morgan Stanley Dean Witter is preparing to introduce an overhaul of its brokerage business and to offer all its clients the option of buying and selling stocks online at discount prices.

The plan, expected to be announced as early as this week, is similar to an offering put forward in June by Merrill Lynch & Co., the country's largest brokerage house. But Morgan Stanley hopes to ambush Merrill by giving all its customers an online trading option immediately, beating Merrill's planned start date by at least six weeks, people close to Morgan Stanley said.

Morgan Stanley already operates Discover Brokerage Direct, an online discount broker. Its new plan envisions eliminating Discover as a separate unit and rolling it together with traditional brokerage services provided by Morgan Stanley's 11,000 full-service brokers. Renamed Morgan Stanley Dean Witter Online, the electronic service will be available either a la carte, for $29.95 a trade, or as part of a full-service brokerage account that carries an annual fee based on assets.

The firm will also take a page from Charles Schwab, the leading online broker, by converting the 450 nationwide branch offices where its brokers work into walk-in retail centers. All its brokerage customers will be able to deposit checks, research stocks, get a consultation or meet with their broker, people close to Morgan Stanley said. A spokesman for the firm declined to comment on any aspect of the plan.

"Morgan Stanley thinks it is really going to be a game of segmenting the market going forward," said Steve Galbraith, an analyst with Sanford C. Bernstein & Co., who said he had heard an outline of the planned overhaul. "They think you have to be able to cater to all segments of the wallet."

The move marks a significant strategic shift by Morgan Stanley that carries several risks. By offering its full-service customers the option of trading online for a fraction of the price they pay in commissions now, Morgan Stanley may suffer a sizable drop in the revenue it gets from commissions, at least in the short term.

Discover brokerage clients will also be slapped with a rare price increase in the ultra-competitive online brokerage business, where Discover has already been losing market share. At $29.95, Morgan Stanley has set its new online commissions to match Schwab and Merrill, making that the high-end benchmark. Discover Brokerage Direct has been charging $14.95 for most stock trades, already higher than the $5 to $8 commissions of rock-bottom online discounters.

People close to Morgan Stanley said that the firm expects Discover—famous for its get-rich-instantly ads featuring a tow-truck driver who owns a tropical island and a schoolboy who flies his own helicopter—to lose some of its online customers when it doubles the cost of trading. But they said many others would pay the higher commissions because Morgan Stanley will now offer them an enriched selection of its stock research and more access to initial public offerings of issues underwritten by its blue-chip investment bank.

"They will pay more, but they will get more," one person close to the firm said.

Morgan Stanley was the first traditional Wall Street firm to dip its toes in the waters of online retail stock trading when it bought Lombard Brokerage, a small San Francisco-based company, in 1996. But it held the operation at arm's length, naming it after its Discover credit card and never integrating it with the firm's much larger full-service operation. Though some Discover customers have had access to Morgan Stanley's highly valued stock research, for example, Morgan Stanley took its name off the research reports and made them available online after a delay to avoid angering full-service brokers and customers.

Morgan Stanley spent tens of millions of dollars promoting the Discover brokerage business on television, in print and online in recent years. That investment seemed predicated in part on the belief that online stock trading was a separate subset of the brokerage business.

Like Merrill Lynch, however, Morgan Stanley has found that online stock trading is more fundamental than that, forcing it to overhaul its operations sooner and more completely than its executives had envisioned only a year ago. People close to Morgan Stanley said that the firm was most worried about the rapid growth of Schwab, which combines inexpensive online trading with efficient call centers and help lines and has lured customers away from all the major brokerage firms.

In some ways Morgan Stanley's overhaul is similar to one that Merrill announced June 1 and expects to finish introducing on December 1. But Morgan Stanley is hoping to steal Merrill's thunder with its coming announcement because it thinks it can offer all its retail brokerage customers access to Discover's online trading platform immediately, while Merrill promoted its plan months before it had prepared the technology to offer the service.

People close to Morgan Stanley also said that the firm expected its plan would cause less internal dissent than was the case at Merrill, where an unusually large number of brokers have defected to rivals since the firm announced its new online trading platform and pricing structure. The key, these people said, is that Morgan Stanley will offer a broad array of pricing options that gives brokers more discretion in how much they charge each customer.

For an asset-based fee of at least $1,500 a year, Merrill Lynch is offering unlimited trading of stocks and bonds either through its brokers or online. Merrill also said it would introduce an online trading service called Merrill Lynch Direct, with individual trades for $29.95. Some Merrill brokers have rebelled because the new pricing structure reduces how much they make from some of their accounts.

Morgan Stanley has addressed that issue by allowing brokers to negotiate prices with customers who want some combination of self-directed online trading and help from a broker. Customers who want such a combination will be charged a percentage of the money they invest with the firm that ranges from less than a half-percent to 2 percent a year. The fees will vary based on the amount of assets and the discretion of the broker involved.

Customers who want to trade online with little or no help from a broker will be charged $29.95 a trade. Full-service customers who do not want to trade online will still have the option of paying higher commissions for broker-directed trading, as they have in the past.

Morgan Stanley's announcement puts fresh pressure on other full-service brokerage houses to make online trading available to all customers who want it. But some rivals say they are not planning to offer deeply discounted stock trading.

The Salomon Smith Barney unit of Citigroup, for example, is planning to introduce online trading by early next month. But the service will be offered only to customers in fee-based or traditional brokerage accounts, not at a discount.

Another traditional brokerage firm, Paine Webber Group, is introducing an account that allows clients who invest at least $100,000 and pay an annual fee to make as many trades as they want, either online or through their brokers. But Paine Webber has not set up a separate online-trading service.

Paine Webber executives stressed that their new account, called Insight One, gave brokers more "flexibility" in pricing brokerage services than Merrill is allowing its brokers. Donald Marron, Paine Webber's chief executive, said the firm kept about $1 annually of every $100 invested with it, and he did not expect that ratio to decline because of the new account.

The New York Times, October 18, 1999
http://www.nytimes.com/library/tech/99/10/biztech/articles/18vamp.html

CRITICAL THINKING QUESTIONS

1. Should Morgan Stanley offer online trading to all its customers? Why, or why not?
2. How will online trading change the job and job prospects for traditional stock-brokers?
3. When compared to online trading, what are the advantages and disadvantages of a traditional stockbroker?

4. How will individuals buy and sell stocks five years from now? How will they be doing it 10 years from now?
5. How safe is Internet stock trading?

STORY-SPECIFIC QUESTIONS

1. What online discount broker does Morgan Stanley already operate?
2. What is one risk that Morgan Stanley faces by offering its full-service customers the option of trading online for a fraction of the price they now pay in commissions?
3. People close to Morgan Stanley said that the firm was most worried about the rapid growth of what brokerage company? Why?
4. What is the key to Morgan Stanley's plan, something that it hopes will cause less internal dissent than was the case at Merrill Lynch, where an unusually large number of brokers have defected to rivals.

SHORT APPLICATION ASSIGNMENTS

1. In teams or individually, answer the story-specific questions; keep your answers to 25–75 words for each question.
2. In teams of three to five persons each, or as a whole class, discuss your responses to the critical thinking questions.
3. Prepare a one-page memo report (200–250 words) to your instructor in which you summarize this article. You will find a model one-page report on the Web site (nytimes.swcollege.com).
4. Write an executive summary (200–250 words). As an administrative assistant to a busy executive, you are expected to summarize selected articles and present important points. You will find a model executive summary on the Web site.
5. Summarize this article (100–125 words) for your company's newsletter. You will find a model newsletter article on the Web site.

BUILDING RESEARCH SKILLS

1. Individually or in teams, compare the Web site of an online broker versus the Web site of a traditional broker. How easy was each site to navigate? What are the requirements for opening an account? What do transactions cost? What services does each site offer? Which brokerage would get your business and why? Your instructor may ask you to submit a three- to five-page essay, post a Web page or report your results in a five-minute presentation, along with a letter of transmittal explaining your findings.
2. Using at least three other references (e.g., books, research-journal articles, newspaper or magazine stories or credible Web sites), write an 800- to 1,000-word essay that addresses two of the critical thinking questions offered earlier. Assume that your essay will be used as an internal reference for a financial institution's investment guidelines.

3. Using at least three other references (e.g., books, research-journal articles, newspaper or magazine stories or credible Web sites), post an 800- to 1,000-word Web page that addresses at least two of the earlier critical thinking questions. Assume that your page will be posted in the investment section of a corporate intranet.

Why Big Firms Are Courting the Day Traders

By David Barboza

Despite growing regulatory concern about the world of day trading, some of the nation's leading investment and securities firms have held talks in recent months with a number of day-trading firms.

Fidelity Investments, Lehman Brothers and Instinet, a division of Reuters Group, have discussed adopting the software platforms of day-trading firms, forming alliances with them or making outright acquisitions, according to several executives who were briefed on the meetings. Executives at the three firms declined to comment on any deal.

Why would big firms want to get involved in such a small industry with a poor reputation and an uncertain future?

The electronic trading boom is forcing them to look for cheaper and more efficient trading formats. Day-trading firms, which in the 1980s and 1990s paved the way to faster and cheaper trading that rankled the powers on Wall Street, now have critical experience developing and using advanced trading and trade-routing software, systems that could someday give all investors instant access to the financial markets.

To be clear, Wall Street firms have little or no interest in the computer-jammed offices where day traders converge to make rapid-fire trades. Instead, they want the software and in some cases the transaction volume generated by these smaller firms.

People briefed on the talks say that the big firms are moving gingerly because of the day-trading industry's recent spate of bad publicity, including the shootings in Atlanta by a disgruntled trader, Mark O. Barton. Just this week, state securities regulators blasted day-trading firms for misleading naïve investors into the risky world of rapid-fire trading.

The day-trading firms at the center of the talks have largely avoided regulatory fines and are best known for their software development and relatively heavy trading volumes. Broadway Trading, Tradescape.com and Cybercorp, all privately held companies, have each been approached in recent months by companies interested in buying a stake or acquiring the firms, executives close to the talks said. The three firms declined to comment.

Although some industry officials warn that Wall Street firms may be talking to day-trading firms simply to gain valuable insights about their technology, a deal between a major broker and one or two day-trading outfits is expected within a few weeks. At least one offer has been made, by Lehman Brothers to acquire Cybercorp, according to someone briefed on the proposal. A major on-line broker is also bidding to acquire a day-trading firm, industry executives said.

"Day trading firms clearly understand the notion of faster, smarter better technology," said Henry H. McVeigh, who covers online brokers at Morgan Stanley Dean Witter. "So while it's taboo to be associated with a day-trading firm, the technology they have is extremely sophisticated and it can be leveraged."

A steady stream of orders to buy and sell stocks is also appealing to some of the bigger firms in the talks. With most financial services companies scrambling to find the right system and the right platform, the number of trading venues has multiplied. The new systems need liquidity, or heavy trading volume, to assure that investors get good prices for their trades. And that is where day-trading firms come in. "The key battle is going to be over order flow," said McVeigh of Morgan Stanley.

Fidelity Investments, a unit of FMR, has said in recent months that it would like to attract more active traders, or those who trade more than 36 times a year. Although its Fidelity Brokerage Services unit has nearly three million accounts, the unit's trading activity lags behind that of E*Trade, which has fewer accounts.

Fidelity executives see faster and more efficient trading systems as a way to attract active investors, though they say they are not searching out day traders. "We talk to a lot of companies about what technology is out there," said Robert P. Mazzarella, president of Fidelity Brokerage Services. "We just launched our active trader Web site. We want to improve the experience and help people trade quicker."

Lehman Brothers, an institutional brokerage firm that has talked to two day-trading firms, is seeking to improve and upgrade its institutional trading systems, executives briefed on the talks said.

Instinet, an electronic network that is a leader in institutional and after-hours trading, said last May that it was interested in breaking into the booming retail market of online trading. It has held talks with Cybercorp and Tradescape.com, according to people briefed on the talks. Such a deal would give Instinet additional day-trading volume for its electronic communications network, which competes against Island E.C.N., a network widely used by day traders and developed by Datek Online Holdings.

Those who have been briefed say that at least one large online broker talked with Broadway Trading in New York about buying all or part of the company before talks broke down. Broadway does not employ its own proprietary software; it uses a platform called the Watcher, which was developed by Datek.

Tradescape.com in New York and Cybercorp in Austin, Texas, are generally considered the most attractive targets, largely because of their software capabilities. Each company has developed proprietary software that can be used on the Internet to trade and get more direct access to the stock market. Tradescape.com recently announced a merger with Momentum Securities in Houston, making it perhaps the nation's largest day-trading firm in trading volume. Softbank, an early investor in E*Trade and Yahoo, recently agreed to invest $40 million in the combined company.

Though executives at Tradescape.com and Cybercorp declined to comment on any talks, they acknowledged that everyone is talking to everyone.

"Some of the largest Wall Street firms recognize they were blind-sided by the electronic execution technology," said Philip Berber, chief executive at Cybercorp. "Primarily these firms want to save themselves two years of time and tens of millions of dollars that it would take to re-create this technology."

They also want to gain order flow at a time when more and more trading activity is taking place outside the purview of major Wall Street brokerage firms or even the major stock exchanges, like the Nasdaq stock market. Electronic communications networks are gobbling up a growing share of the marketplace, and firms want to make sure they do not miss out. The firms say they have technology that works with E.C.N.'s to hunt for the best price.

In turning to day-trading firms, the major Wall Street firms are imitating a model developed by Datek Online, which got its start as a day-trading firm and later developed fast execution and trade-routing technology that spawned the Island E.C.N., which is heavily used by Broadway Trading, Tradescape.com and Heartland Securities, a day-trading unit that was spun off of Datek in 1998 amid regulatory questions and investigations of its trading practices.

Still, Datek is considered a pioneer in developing technology for day trading and transferring that technology to more mainstream applications, a knack that has made it one of the nation's fastest growing online brokerage firms.

Day trading, which has been driven by the opportunity of fantastic profits during a stunning bull market, now appears to be evolving again. Wall Street analysts and day-trading officials say many former professional traders, brokers and financial services professionals are quitting their jobs to work full time as day traders or money managers from home offices.

Most people with online accounts now e-mail an order to the online broker, who then routes the order, often selling it to Wall Street wholesalers, who execute the trades. The future lies in faster, cheaper, quicker access to the markets, which will create a bulge in online brokers. Perhaps, the technology visionaries say, online brokerage firms will then hire sales forces and money managers, who can work from home offices trading accounts for their customers. It would be a virtual retail brokerage firm.

The whole concept of direct access to the markets is coming out of day trading, said James H. Lee, head of the Electronic Traders Association and president of Momentum Securities. "That's why we see some of this hysteria," he said. "It rocks right to the core of the Wall Street establishment."

The New York Times, August 13, 1999
http://www.nytimes.com/library/tech/99/08/biztech/articles/13place.html

CRITICAL THINKING QUESTIONS

1. How safe is Internet stock trading?
2. What governmental agencies should regulate Internet stock trading? How should each agency regulate Internet stock trading?
3. What is day trading?
4. Is day trading best suited for experienced investors? Why, or why not?
5. Why would big firms want to get involved in such a small industry with a poor reputation and an uncertain future?
6. Will the big, traditional firms eventually gobble up the smaller day-trading firms? Explain.

STORY-SPECIFIC QUESTIONS

1. While big Wall Street firms have little interest in the computer-jammed offices where day traders converge to make rapid-fire trades, what does attract them to these smaller firms?
2. What three firms have discussed adopting the software platforms of day-trading firms, forming alliances with them or making outright acquisitions?
3. What is Instinet and what does it do?
4. What possible scenario for retail brokerage firms do technology visionaries predict?

SHORT APPLICATION ASSIGNMENTS

1. In teams or individually, answer the story-specific questions; keep your answers to 25–75 words for each question.
2. In teams of three to five persons each, or as a whole class, discuss your responses to the critical thinking questions.
3. Prepare a one-page memo report (200–250 words) to your instructor in which you summarize this article. You will find a model one-page report on the Web site (nytimes.swcollege.com).
4. Write an executive summary (200–250 words). As an administrative assistant to a busy executive, you are expected to summarize selected articles and present important points. You will find a model executive summary on the Web site.
5. Summarize this article (100–125 words) for your company's newsletter. You will find a model newsletter article on the Web site.
6. Read Matthew Klam's account of a day trader "Riding the Mo In the Lime Green Glow" (http://www.nytimes.com/library/magazine/home/19991121mag-klam.html). Your instructor may ask you to present the article in an oral report or submit a 150- to 200-word summary.
7. Read Gretchen Morgenstern's "Regulators Seek More Accountability From Online Trading Firms" (http://www.nytimes.com/library/tech/99/11/biztech/articles/23online.html). Your instructor may ask you to present the article in an oral report or submit a 150- to 200-word summary.

BUILDING RESEARCH SKILLS

1. Individually or in teams, compare three of the following Web sites: Datek (http://www.datek.com/), Instinet (http://www.instinet.com/), Tradescape (http://www.tradescape.com/), Cybercorp (http://www.cybercorp.com/) and Fidelity (http://www.fidelity.com/). Topics to consider on each Web site include ease of navigation, services offered, pricing, target customers and alliances. Your instructor may ask you to submit a three- to five-page essay, post a Web page or report your results in a five-minute presentation, along with a letter of transmittal explaining your findings.

2. Using at least three other references (e.g., books, research-journal articles, newspaper or magazine stories or credible Web sites), write an 800- to 1,000-word essay that addresses two of the critical thinking questions offered earlier. Assume that your essay will be used as an internal reference for a financial institution's investment guidelines.

3. Using at least three other references (e.g., books, research-journal articles, newspaper or magazine stories or credible Web sites), post an 800- to 1,000-word Web page that addresses at least two of the earlier critical thinking questions. Assume that your page will be posted in the investment section of a corporate intranet.

Attacks on Encryption Code Raise Questions About Computer Vulnerability

By Peter Wayner

Members of the computer security industry—the folks who keep credit card numbers safe from prying eyes on the Internet, among other things—can be a contentious bunch. Competition, after all, often consists of trying to break the other guy's code-scrambling technology in order to sell a fix or alternative product.

But even by those standards, the industry is girding for an especially nasty fight when the annual RSA conference is held early this month.

RSA, the public key encryption algorithm named for Ronald Rivest, Adi Shamir, and Leonard Adleman, who invented it in 1978, is the foundation on which much of the security protecting consumers and merchants on the World Wide Web has been built.

Those systems are under constant assault by security experts, competitors and hackers alike.

In recent months, several widely used encryption technologies, including one used to scramble cell-phone conversations, have been cracked or at least seriously threatened—all by security experts in the name of protecting data.

Among the more interesting recent attacks is one created by nCipher, a small British company that makes special hardware it says can encrypt information faster and more securely than a typical computer can. One of its scientists, Nicko van Someren, recently demonstrated a simple program that can extract the secret keys locked in a Web server used to process credit card transactions. It is one of the first practical demonstrations of a theoretical approach to code breaking that Mr. van Someren developed about 18 months ago with Mr. Shamir, the Israeli cryptography expert who is the "S" in RSA.

The attack is cause for concern because someone with a company's secret keys—the digital codes that unscramble data—can use the information to masquerade as that company and to steal credit card numbers and other financial data.

"While the merchants running the servers are the targets, the customers are the victims," says Alex van Someren, Nicko's brother and the chief executive of nCipher. "If the Web servers are compromised, ultimately the financially sensitive information that's going to be lost belongs to a customer."

Indeed, the nCipher attack could hurt small merchants the most because as a matter of economy, they often share Web servers, the big computers that operate Web pages, with other merchants.

Until recently, many experts assumed that the casual barriers separating various companies' Web sites on the same server were more than adequate.

This attack, however, circumvents those barriers by loading a special version of a program that merchants on the same Web server typically share. Known as a C.G.I., for "Common Gateway Interface," this program's job is to record the details of a transaction and send back customized messages to consumers thanking them for their orders.

Mr. van Someren demonstrated that a C.G.I. could be written in such a way that it evades the thin walls of security that separate companies on the same server and identifies secret keys. The attack works against most operating systems that power Web servers, including the Microsoft Corporation's Windows NT and Windows 2000 and Sun Microsystems' Solaris.

One of the more novel elements of the attack is the fact that it works blindly. While the C.G.I. can slip around the barriers and read data stored in the server's memory, it receives no clues as to what the data means.

So how does it find the secret keys hidden among all the other scrambled data? Paradoxically, by spotting the very randomness that makes data-scrambling secure in the first place.

Mr. Van Someren and Mr. Shamir found that the keys are substantially more random than most other data. Alphanumeric text—the letters and numerals consumers give to Web sites, for instance—is generally repetitious and rife with patterns. And since text is typically represented by numbers between 32 and 127, Mr. Someren's program scans the server's memory looking for data that include all possible numbers with no concentration of any particular value.

Not coincidentally, nCipher makes a product that defends against attacks, so it is in the company's best interest to warn online merchants about the malicious C.G.I. it created. NCipher also published details of the program, making it easier for hackers to duplicate—thus making e-commerce sites more vulnerable to attack and more likely to buy nCipher's product.

While this kind of activity might be deemed unethical in many other lines of work, it's considered fair game in the security industry.

"Is it blackmail?" said Alex van Someren. "The key issue here is we have to break the systems here to make them stronger. You need to understand how people break in to keep them out."

Besides, he argued, keeping the company's knowledge about the attack a secret might have been even more unethical. Publishing a general warning, he noted, at least made it possible for Web masters to defend their sites.

He added that online merchants were free to adopt any number of defenses, including solutions from nCipher's rivals.

To be sure, nCipher is not the only company that makes specialized hardware for encrypting and decrypting credit card numbers and other sensitive information. IBM and other companies specializing in electronic commerce offer competing products and are constantly engaged in researching the technology.

And in general, security hardware that is separate from the server computer offers an advantage because it removes the keys from the scrambled data, making them unavailable to hackers who find a way around a server's security systems.

Peter Neumann, a computer security researcher at SRI International in Menlo Park, California, says that such hardware is a wise investment because Microsoft and other makers of operating systems have done little to plug security holes in their products.

"We knew how to solve many of these problems in the 1960s," Mr. Neumann said, "but we've lost all of that in the mainstream."

Robert Hettinga, chief executive of Internet Bearer Underwriting Corporation, which employs several kinds of cryptography to protect Internet transactions, said the best solution might be a sort of cyberspace isolationism. Computer systems are becoming so cheap, he said, that most companies should be able to avoid sharing a server.

The C.G.I. attack, Mr. Hettinga said, proves that these days, "sharing a digital commerce server is like sharing someone's toothbrush."

The New York Times, January 5, 2000
http://www.nytimes.com/library/tech/00/01/biztech/articles/05secu.html

CRITICAL THINKING QUESTIONS

1. Has encryption made Internet transactions safe? Why, or why not?
2. Is it safe to give one's credit card number over the Internet? Why, or why not?
3. Are attacks on encryption code a form of blackmail or a public service? Explain.
4. How will encryption evolve over the next five years? Over the next 10 years?
5. How vulnerable are e-commerce Web sites to attacks by hackers?

STORY-SPECIFIC QUESTIONS

1. What is RSA? Who invented RSA? What does it do?
2. Why is nCipher's recent attack cause for concern?
3. How could the nCipher attack hurt small merchants the most?
4. Hettinga compares sharing a digital commerce server to sharing what personal product?

SHORT APPLICATION ASSIGNMENTS

1. In teams or individually, answer the story-specific questions; keep your answers to 25–75 words for each question.
2. In teams of three to five persons each, or as a whole class, discuss your responses to the critical thinking questions.

3. Prepare a one-page memo report (200–250 words) to your instructor in which you summarize this article. You will find a model one-page report on the Web site (nytimes.swcollege.com).

4. Write an executive summary (200–250 words). As an administrative assistant to a busy executive, you are expected to summarize selected articles and present important points. You will find a model executive summary on the Web site.

5. Summarize this article (100–125 words) for your company's newsletter. You will find a model newsletter article on the Web site.

6. Individually or in teams, research the encryption and security policy of an e-commerce Web site. Did the site have a policy? Would you give your credit card number to this site? What technology, if any, did the site use? Your instructor may assign you an e-commerce site or you may choose one. Your instructor may also ask you to present your findings in an oral report or submit a 150- to 200-word summary.

BUILDING RESEARCH SKILLS

1. Individually or in teams, compare the encryption products offered on two of the following Web sites: IBM (http://www.ibm.com/), RSA (http://www.rsasecurity.com/) and nCipher (http://www.ncipher.com). Who is their target customer? What are their competitive advantages? What have their recent press releases trumpeted? What do you like, or dislike about their encryption products? Your instructor may ask you to submit a three- to five-page essay, post a Web page or report your results in a five-minute presentation, along with a letter of transmittal explaining your findings.

2. Individually or in teams, review the various conferences listed at the RSA (http://www.rsasecurity.com/) Web site. Topics to consider include the conference exhibitors, sponsors, participants and topics. Your instructor may ask you to submit a three- to five-page essay or report your results in a five-minute presentation, along with a letter of transmittal explaining your findings.

3. Using at least three other references (e.g., books, research-journal articles, newspaper or magazine stories or credible Web sites), write an 800- to 1,000-word essay that addresses two of the critical thinking questions offered earlier. Assume that your essay will be used as an internal reference for a financial institution's security guidelines.

4. Using at least three other references (e.g., books, research-journal articles, newspaper or magazine stories or credible Web sites), post an 800- to 1,000-word Web page that addresses at least two of the earlier critical thinking questions. Assume that your page will be posted in the security section of a corporate intranet.

Financial Management
in the Corporate Environment

PREVIEW

At the corporate level, financial managers walk a fine line, balancing the interests of the board of directors, stockholders, customers and employees. At times, their decisions may not please all parties. Dividend policy, pension planning, and mergers and acquisitions are a few of the many hard choices that corporate financial managers must ponder.

Was America Online's offer to purchase Time Warner a sound financial decision for AOL? For Time Warner? Saul Hansell reports on the steps leading up to, and the factors behind, one of the biggest financial decisions ever made in "America Online to Buy Time Warner for $165 Billion."

Shareholders in Time Warner currently receive a dividend on the stock they own, but not so for owners of AOL stock. While dividends were once necessary to entice buyers to a corporation's stock, this may no longer be the case. Floyd Norris explores a recent trend in "Growing Number of Companies Choose Not to Offer Dividends."

Pensions are another corporate expenditure aimed at keeping individuals—employees, not stockholders—happy. But as Richard A. Oppel Jr. explains in "Under Fire, IBM Alters Pension Plan," there is no simple financial solution for keeping a smile on employees' faces.

Stephen M. Case, left, chief of America Online; Gerald M. Levin, chief of Time Warner; Ted Turner, vice chairman of Time; Robert Pittman, chief operating officer of AOL; Richard Parsons, president of Time; and J. Michael Kelly, chief financial officer of AOL, at Monday's news conference.

Source: Angel Franco/The New York Times

America Online to Buy Time Warner for $165 Billion

By Saul Hansell

America Online, the company that brought the Internet to the masses, said yesterday that it had agreed to buy the largest traditional media company, Time Warner, for $165 billion in what would be the biggest merger in history and the best evidence yet that old and new media are converging.

By agreeing to give up its independence in return for an ample premium on its stock price, Time Warner is acknowledging that the Internet is central to its music, publishing and TV businesses and that its own efforts to create online operations have been lackluster. Under the direction of its 41-year-old chairman and chief executive, Stephen M. Case, America Online, despite the occasional stumble, has surged far ahead of its online competitors, largely on the strength of its marketing skill and ability to make technology easy to use.

America Online, in turn, would gain access to Time Warner's entertainment and information empire. And of more immediate importance would be that the company—whose 22 million paying subscribers now use modems and telephone lines to go online—would get access to Time Warner's cable television systems.

Those systems, which now serve 13 million subscribers, would enable America Online to start offering much speedier Internet and interactive television services. Until this deal, no major cable company would carry America Online's services.

The new offerings might include Internet versions of Time Warner's media properties, like news from CNN or movies from Home Box Office, combined with a range of features more sophisticated than the Web sites, chat rooms and e-mail services that are now staples of America Online.

The earliest impact might come in music, where America Online is already developing technology for a digital jukebox that could store and play songs from Warner Music and other labels.

And for consumers generally, whether they now or ever subscribe to America Online or Time Warner services, yesterday's announcement is very likely to portend other mergers and alliances that could hasten the development of and availability of high-capacity information and entertainment networks.

The deal, which was negotiated with such secrecy that it took the industry by surprise, also brought a new realization about the extraordinary stock-market values that America Online and other Internet companies have reached the last 18 months. Although analysts have long predicted that the stars among the Internet upstarts would wind up part of larger media empires, the deal indicates that it could be the Internet companies that do the buying and the old media that sell out.

"The dot-com guys have sort of won," said David B. Readerman, an analyst with Thomas Weisel Partners, a San Francisco brokerage firm. "AOL was able to serve up its stock and buy Time Warner, walking away with incredible media assets."

Another winner is Mr. Case, who is to become the chairman of the new company, which would be called AOL Time Warner. Time Warner's current chairman and chief executive, Gerald M. Levin, 60, would serve under Mr. Case as the new company's chief executive.

With a market value of $342 billion, based on yesterday's closing stock prices, the combined corporation would be the fourth-most-valuable company in the country, after Microsoft, General Electric and Cisco Systems. And its stock market value would roughly be equal to the gross domestic product of Mexico.

Besides requiring the approval of both companies' shareholders, the combination will face the usual review by antitrust regulators as well as a complex web of local reviews as cable television franchises are transferred into America Online's name. It will also require review by Federal antitrust regulators. The Clinton administration has not yet decided whether to refer the matter to the Justice Department, which has examined America Online's past acquisitions, or to the Federal Trade Commission, which approved the merger between Time and Warner Communications 10 years ago.

Although some consumer groups and members of Congress called for careful scrutiny of the merger, the companies said they did not expect any problems because their businesses do not overlap and neither company dominates its respective markets. No other Internet-access provider, however, has more than about a tenth as many customers as America Online. The companies said they hoped to close the deal by the end of the year.

Mr. Case was already a billionaire but not the instant sort created by some of the newer Internet companies—many of which, unlike America Online, have never achieved a profit. America Online became profitable in 1998 and has earned $879 million in the last four quarters, on sales of $5.2 billion, far more than any other Internet company. Mr. Case worked for 15 years, through obscurity and ridicule, to achieve his vision that chatting on a computer screen would become as important a communications medium as the telephone or television.

It was Mr. Case who proposed the combination last October to Mr. Levin, winning an initial hearing by offering him the chief executive's title in the combined company. After much haggling over the financial terms, the deal was cemented at a five-hour meeting at Mr. Case's house in Northern Virginia on Thursday night.

As measured by its revenue in the last 12 months of $27.7 billion, Time Warner is already the largest of the conventional media companies. (But the

Time Inc. publishing division, on which Henry Luce founded the company with *Time* magazine nearly 70 years ago, would represent less than 15 percent of AOL Time Warner's revenue.) If the merger is completed, the new company would be an even more powerful player in a wide range of industries.

AT&T, which is in the process of becoming the largest owner of cable television systems, would face a more formidable America Online, which had been trying to gain access to AT&T's cable systems. And Microsoft would be contending with an even bigger rival as computer software continues to evolve into Internet-based services—a field in which America Online has excelled.

Indeed, in light of yesterday's announcement, analysts and executives were quick to predict that more media and technology companies would run to the altar.

"The combination of old and new media companies will happen far faster because of this," said George Bell, the president of Excite@Home, the company controlled by AT&T that offers high-speed Internet services over cable systems. "Fundamentally, Time Warner has something AOL doesn't have: great media brands built up over decades. The time isn't there for Internet companies to build that content. Time just won't hold still."

By the same reasoning, other media companies might see the virtue in finding a partner with Internet competence—as did Time Warner, whose decision to sell out is a tacit admission that the biggest and most talented publishers and studio executives have been at a loss to figure out how to apply their talents to new media. Time Warner was an early player in interactive television, through the Full Service Network, an expensive prototype it introduced in Orlando, Florida. And its Pathfinder service, one of the pioneering sites on the World Wide Web, was never able to turn the company's substantial brands like *Time* and *Sports Illustrated* into a major force.

Few of the other media companies have done any better online. Only Walt Disney, with its Go Network, is among the 10 top Internet services.

The big cable operators, including AT&T and Time Warner, have long wanted to be the exclusive Internet providers on the systems they own. But America Online has been calling for open access—the ability to offer a high-speed service over any cable system just as it offers its current service through the wires of any telephone company.

In yesterday's announcement, Time Warner pledged to support open access to its cable systems by any Internet provider. In practice, neither of the merger partners would have much business incentive to deal exclusively only with each other. Were America Online to restrict itself only to Time Warner's 13-million-subscriber cable systems, it would be missing the opportunity to serve the tens of millions of other people already on the Internet who might be willing to sign up for a new, high-speed AOL.

The man who started CNN two decades ago, was Ted Turner, Time Warner's 61-year-old vice chairman and its largest shareholder. Yesterday, Mr. Turner explained his support for the merger.

SIGNING UP A NEW GIANT

The merger of AOL and Time Warner will combine elements of traditional media and new media to create a company with holdings in a broad range of industries.

Internet

AOL is the Internet's leading service provider, reaching more than 22 million members through AOL and Compuserve. Those members spend on average nearly an hour online every day. Its ICQ and A.I.M. instant messaging services are use by 100 million people. AOL purchased Netscape, creator of the original Internet browser, in the fall of 1998.

Cable Systems

The country's second largest operator of cable television systems, Time Warner Cable has 13 million customers. More than 80 percent of these are in the 33 markets shown below.

Publishing

Time Warner's stable of 33 magazines had 120 million readers last year, and accounted for 21 percent of all consumer magazine advertising revenue in 1998. It sold $1.1 billion worth of books through Book-of-the-Month Club and Time Life and Little, Brown and Warner Books in 1998.

Magazines

Time	Cooking Light	People
Baby Talk	Sports Illustrated	Coastal Living
Fortune	Health	Life
Progressive Farmer	Money	Southern Living
Parenting	This Old House	In Style
Teen People	Entertainment Weekly	Wallpaper

Books

Book-of-the-Month Club	Sunset Books	Little Brown
Oxmoor House	Warner Books	Leisure Arts
Time Life		

Television Broadcasting

CNN, the TBS Superstation, TNT and CNN all reach more than 70 million cable subscribers in the United States. HBO and Cinemax, premium channels, reach 35 million subscribers.

Cable Channels

CNN	CNNfn	TBS	Turner Classic Movies
HBO	CINEMAX	TNT	NY1
Cartoon Network	The WB		

continued

Movie and Television Production
Produces both television shows, like ER, The Rosie O'Donnell Show and the Sopranos for HBO and movies through Warner Bros. and New Line Cinema.

Recent Movies

Warner Bros.
Any Given Sunday
L.A. Confidential
The Matrix
Wild Wild West
Austin Powers: The Spy Who
   Shagged Me

Analyze This
Eyes Wide Shut
The Iron Giant
You've Got Mail
New Line Cinema
Rush Hour

Television

Warner Bros.
The Drew Carey Show
HBO
The Sopranos

Friends
Dawson's Creek
Sex and the City

"When I cast my vote for 100 million shares, I did it with as much excitement as I felt the first time I made love some 42 years ago," Mr. Turner said. "I voted for it because we will have a stronger company that will create value. It's not so easy to go out and recreate AOL. No one has been able to do it so far."

The New York Times, January 11, 2000
http://www.nytimes.com/library/financial/011100time-aol.html

CRITICAL THINKING QUESTIONS

1. Was this a merger of equals? Why, or why not?
2. As an investor in Time Warner, would you favor or oppose this merger? Explain.
3. As an investor in America Online, would you favor or oppose this merger? Explain.
4. As a consumer, would you favor or oppose this merger? Explain.

STORY-SPECIFIC QUESTIONS

1. What was the combined value of the two companies?
2. Briefly describe Time Warner's publishing empire.
3. By agreeing to give up its independence in return for an ample premium on its stock price, what is Time Warner acknowledging?
4. Who is Time Warner's largest shareholder and how many shares does this person own?

SHORT APPLICATION ASSIGNMENTS

1. In teams or individually, answer the story-specific questions; keep your answers to 25–75 words for each question.
2. In teams of three to five persons each, or as a whole class, discuss your responses to the critical thinking questions.
3. Prepare a one-page memo report (200–250 words) to your instructor in which you summarize this article. You will find a model one-page report on the Web site (nytimes.swcollege.com).
4. Write an executive summary (200–250 words). As an administrative assistant to a busy executive, you are expected to summarize selected articles and present important points. You will find a model executive summary on the Web site.
5. Summarize this article (100–125 words) for your company's newsletter. You will find a model newsletter article on the Web site.
6. Individually or in teams, chart the value of Time Warner and America Online's stock since the merger.
7. Read "Mass Medium for Main Street and Huge Victory for AOL," which is linked to this story. Your instructor may ask you to present your findings in an oral report or submit a 150- to 200-word summary.

BUILDING RESEARCH SKILLS

1. Individually or in teams, research a merger that happened four or more years ago. Did this merger benefit shareholders? Why, or why not? Your instructor may assign you a merger or you may choose one. Your instructor may also ask you to submit a three- to five-page essay, post a Web page or report your results in a five-minute presentation, along with a letter of transmittal explaining your findings.
2. Individually or in teams, research the proposed MCI Worldcom-Sprint merger. The following story, "MCI Worldcom to Acquire Sprint in Stock Swap Valued at $108 Billion" (http://www.nytimes.com/library/financial/100599sprint-merger.html) may help you. Did this merger benefit shareholders? Why, or why not? Your instructor may assign you a merger or you may choose one. Your instructor may also ask you to submit a three- to five-page essay, post a Web page or report your results in a five-minute presentation, along with a letter of transmittal explaining your findings.
3. Using at least three other references (e.g., books, research-journal articles, newspaper or magazine stories or credible Web sites), write an 800- to 1,000-word essay that addresses two of the critical thinking questions offered earlier. Assume that your essay will be used as an internal reference for a financial institution's investment guidelines.
4. Using at least three other references (e.g., books, research-journal articles, newspaper or magazine stories or credible Web sites), post an 800- to 1,000-word Web page that addresses at least two of the earlier critical thinking questions. Assume that your page will be posted in the investment section of a corporate intranet.

Growing Number of Companies Choose Not to Offer Dividends

By Floyd Norris

A growing portion of corporate America appears to be concluding that dividends are no longer needed to attract investors and are therefore an unnecessary cost of doing business. Fewer companies are raising dividends, and more and more major companies do not bother to pay them at all.

Dividends used to be a virtual requirement to convince investors that a company was successful and worthy of investment. Some institutional investors were barred from buying stocks that did not pay dividends.

But now, for the first time in recent history—and probably the first time since the Depression—a quarter of the value of the Standard & Poor's index of 500 stocks comes from companies that do not pay dividends. Two decades ago, only 2 percent of the value of the index came from such companies.

In those days, a company in the S&P 500 that did not pay a dividend probably had been forced to stop doing so because of financial problems. These days, however, dividends are out of favor, and it is the hottest companies that don't pay them.

"At one time, stocks were considered riskier than other asset classes, so they had to pay dividends," said Arnold Kaufman, the editor of the *Outlook* newsletter published by Standard & Poor's. But now, he said, investors see stocks as less risky, and thus do not demand such protection.

While 402 of the 500 stocks in the index did pay dividends last year, only one of the top 15 performers, and 14 of the top 50, did so. Of the 14 that paid dividends, only one—Morgan Stanley Dean Witter—is paying out at least 1 percent of its share value. Since the company's share price doubled last year, that payout obviously made up a very small portion of the shareholder return.

Most of the companies in the S&P 500 that are not paying dividends are successful technology companies that have profits, not hot Internet start-ups. The five largest non-dividend payers in the S&P—Microsoft, Cisco, America Online, Oracle and MCI WorldCom—are all profitable and have never paid dividends.

Apple Computer, however, never resumed paying dividends after it halted them when it encountered financial difficulties in the mid-1990s.

As recently as 1997, 90 percent of the value of the index came from companies that paid dividends. But that fell to 85.2 percent in 1998 and to 74.8 percent last year.

To some extent, the decline reflects the fact that the S&P has been more willing to add technology stocks that do not pay dividends to the index. But it also reflects an investor attitude that puts little pressure on companies to make payouts. While companies can still be penalized for reducing or eliminating dividends, they get little credit for introducing or raising dividends.

To be sure, most companies still pay dividends, and many raise their payouts every year. But the trend is unmistakable. Standard & Poor's reported yesterday that 1,701 dividend increases were reported by American companies last year, or 16.9 percent fewer than in 1998. There were smaller declines in 1997 and 1998.

In the past, a sharp decline of 15 percent or more in the number of companies with dividend increases usually came during recessions, when many companies were financially strapped. But the latest downtrend has come as the economy has boomed. The only similar trend occurred in the late 1960s, another time that small technology companies were all the rage and the market for new issues was red hot. Some of the hot issues of that era, such as Electronic Data Systems, became successful, but most did not.

A variety of reasons are given for the trend away from dividends, including the tax disadvantages. Dividends are taxable to investors as ordinary income but are not deductible from corporate income, and thus face double taxation. But that has always been true, and the effect presumably should have been greater two decades ago, when tax rates were much higher. Some companies say they instead return money to shareholders by repurchasing shares, allowing the sellers to pay lower capital gains tax rates on the money. But in many cases those purchases only offset the shares being issued to employees who exercise options.

One explanation is that corporate officials are far more likely than in the past to have a large part of their wealth in stock options. Such options become more valuable as the stock price rises, but do not benefit from dividend payments, arguably providing an incentive to companies not to pay dividends. Moreover, if a company runs into a cash squeeze, cutting back on share repurchases is far less obvious than reducing dividends.

The most likely explanation, however, would seem to be the most obvious. Investors, after seeing year after year of huge capital gains, no longer see much of a need for dividends as an assured return if the market declines.

The best performing stock in the S&P 500 to pay a dividend last year was Nortel Networks, which ranked fifth in performance with a gain of 304 percent. It last raised its dividend in 1997, when its stock price was one-fifth of today's level. At its current payout rate of 3.75 cents a quarter, Nortel stock yields 0.15 percent a year.

The trend toward lower dividends can be seen in the overall dividend yield on the S&P 500. Once it was a rule of thumb that caution was warranted if stock prices rose so high that the dividend yield fell below 3 percent. At the height in 1987, before that year's crash, the yield had fallen below 2.65 percent, then a record low yield.

But the yield on the S&P 500 last year, based on payouts by the companies during the year and the year-end level of the index, came to just 1.14 percent, down from 1.32 percent in 1998 and 1.6 percent in 1997. The rate has been below 3 percent since 1991, as the stock market recorded its best decade ever.

The New York Times, January 2, 2000
http://www.nytimes.com/library/financial/010400dividends-marketplace.html

CRITICAL THINKING QUESTIONS

1. For the corporation, what are the advantages and disadvantages of paying dividends to shareholders?
2. For the investor, what are the advantages and disadvantages of investing in a stock that pays a dividend?
3. Will more companies choose not to offer dividends?
4. As an investor, why would you prefer, or not prefer, stocks that pay dividends?

STORY-SPECIFIC QUESTIONS

1. What are the five largest non-dividend paying corporations in the Standard & Poor's index of 500 stocks?
2. In the last two decades, how have companies that do not pay dividends increased their value in the Standard & Poor's index of 500 stocks?
3. What does Arnold Kaufman offer as an early reason that stocks paid dividends?
4. What was the rule of thumb concerning stock prices and dividend yields?

SHORT APPLICATION ASSIGNMENTS

1. In teams or individually, answer the story-specific questions; keep your answers to 25–75 words for each question.
2. In teams of three to five persons each, or as a whole class, discuss your responses to the critical thinking questions.
3. Prepare a one-page memo report (200–250 words) to your instructor in which you summarize this article. You will find a model one-page report on the Web site (nytimes.swcollege.com).
4. Write an executive summary (200–250 words). As an administrative assistant to a busy executive, you are expected to summarize selected articles and present important points. You will find a model executive summary on the Web site.
5. Summarize this article (100–125 words) for your company's newsletter. You will find a model newsletter article on the Web site.

BUILDING RESEARCH SKILLS

1. Individually or in teams, research and compare four publicly traded companies that have paid dividends over the last ten years. How often do they pay the dividend?

Has the dividend changed? Has the yield percentage changed? Has the company consistently paid the stated dividend? Your instructor may ask you to submit a three- to five-page essay, post a Web page or report your results in a five-minute presentation, along with a letter of transmittal explaining your findings.

2. Using at least three other references (e.g., books, research-journal articles, newspaper or magazine stories or credible Web sites), write an 800- to 1,000-word essay that addresses two of the critical thinking questions offered earlier. Assume that your essay will be used as an internal reference for a financial institution's investment guidelines.

3. Using at least three other references (e.g., books, research-journal articles, newspaper or magazine stories or credible Web sites), post an 800- to 1,000-word Web page that addresses at least two of the earlier critical thinking questions. Assume that your page will be posted in the investment section of a corporate intranet.

Under Fire, IBM Alters Pension Plan

By Richard A. Oppel Jr.

In a major victory for opponents of a controversial type of new pension, IBM said Friday that it would allow 35,000 additional employees to retain their old pension benefits, backing down from an earlier move forcing them to accept what for many would be far lower benefits from a new "cash balance" pension.

The company has been under pressure since it announced earlier this year that it was switching to a cash-balance plan, prompting lawmakers to demand age-discrimination investigations and IBM workers to seek to organize a union.

The International Business Machines Corporation, based in Armonk, New York, is one of hundreds of large companies that have switched from traditional pension plans to cash-balance pensions. In the old plans, employees earned most of their retirement benefits toward the end of their careers, but under cash-balance plans, employees accrue benefits equally over their career. As a result, younger workers see their pensions grow faster, but older workers can lose a significant amount of benefits.

That has prompted protests by middle-aged workers at a number of companies, but most notably IBM, where furious employees used Internet sites to organize rallies.

Even with the change, some IBM employees will still be forced to accept the cash-balance pension whether or not they want to. But the reversal more than doubles—to 65,000—the employees who can choose to keep their old pension benefits. Many middle-aged IBM employees had said they would lose one-fifth to one-half of their benefits because of the change, and IBM had even said that 45,000 employees who had worked at the company for 15 to 24 years would see average benefit reductions of 20 percent, assuming early retirement.

But with the about-face, any employee at least 40 years old and with a decade of service—as of June 30—will be allowed to opt for either plan.

Tom Bouchard, IBM's senior vice president for human resources, said in an e-mail to employees Friday: "We've heard from thousands of IBMers, many of whom expressed deep concerns about how the changes would affect their families and their long-term financial planning. While some of what was expressed was not very productive, most of the comments we received were thoughtful, professional and very insightful."

He continued: "We looked at whether we could extend the choice of which plan to select to more people, without compromising IBM's competitive position. We've decided that we can."

Lawmakers and others involved in the fight said the reversal, along with other developments this week favorable to cash-balance opponents, would embolden workers elsewhere to fight similar changes.

The Equal Employment Opportunity Commission said it would investigate whether conversions to cash-balance plans discriminate illegally against older workers.

The Internal Revenue Service also said it was examining the issue and had delayed approvals of pension conversions.

Representative Bernard Sanders, an Independent from Vermont and opponent of cash-balance conversions, said the reversal "shows when workers stand together, they can have a major impact, even against institutions as powerful as IBM."

He added, "What IBM has essentially said is that we do not want to be accused of being in violation of age-discrimination laws, and I think that should send a very clear signal to other companies interested in doing what IBM did."

Senator James M. Jeffords, Republican of Vermont, whose committee will hold a hearing on the issue Tuesday, said the chief executive of IBM, Louis V. Gerstner Jr., telephoned him with the news Friday morning. "He recognized he had a problem, obviously, from the employees' reaction, and he listened to his employees," Jeffords said.

IBM has maintained that the conversion is legal and does not discriminate against any workers. Jana Weatherbee, a spokeswoman, denied that pressure by any outside forces—union organizers, lawmakers, Federal agencies or anyone else—prompted the move.

"We rethought what we had done because of what our employees were telling us," Ms. Weatherbee said. "This is a question of balance, the need to balance the needs of employees with what we can afford from a competitive point of view. This strikes the right balance."

IBM had previously said the switch would save $200 million a year, which would go to other employee compensation. "We never did this to save money," she said. "The change will have a cost to IBM, but the exact amount will depend on how many people choose the new plan versus stay in the old one."

While many IBM employees rejoiced over the news, some want to see the fine print. "I trust what they said. I just want to see details of the plan," said Bill Syverson, an IBM engineer in Essex Junction, Vermont. "They're still missing people under 40. IBM finally showed some positive movement, but I remain skeptical until I hear the full story."

Phil Nigh, a 38-year-old worker at the Essex Junction plant, said he was happy for his older colleagues but that he estimated that he would lose about one-quarter of his pension because he did not make the new cutoff. "What happened was this went from being really, really unfair to just unfair," said Nigh, who has spent 16 years at IBM "It's a relative thing."

The reversal also showed the new power that the Internet has brought to employee organizing. As anger over the pension changes mounted, employees across the country plotted strategy and organized rallies and other protests using the Internet.

Lynda French, an IBM employee in Austin, Texas, whose husband, also an IBM employee, had just missed qualifying for the old pension under the prior cutoff, started a Web site at www.cashpensions.com.

"The power of the Internet is just phenomenal," Ms. French said. "This was the only way employees could get educated on the subject."

She added that before Friday's announcement her husband stood to lose 37 percent of his pension. "We were frantic," she said.

The New York Times, September 18, 1999
http://www.nytimes.com/library/tech/99/09/biztech/articles/18pension.html

CRITICAL THINKING QUESTIONS

1. How does a corporation balance financial and human resource decisions?
2. Changes in benefits often affect older employees more adversely than their younger counterparts. Why should younger employees join their older colleagues in fighting back?
3. Should IBM have backed down? Why, or why not?
4. What type of pension plan would make sense for both older and younger employees?
5. Do the benefits of pension plans offset the costs of pension plans? Why, or why not?
6. What criteria should be used to determine eligibility and benefits of a corporate pension plan?

STORY-SPECIFIC QUESTIONS

1. How did angry IBM employees fight back to save their pensions?
2. Besides employees, who else became involved in the battle to save the traditional pension plan?
3. What is the difference between traditional pension plans and cash-balance plans?
4. What effect would the cash-balance plan have had on older IBM employees, and how much money would it have saved IBM?

SHORT APPLICATION ASSIGNMENTS

1. In teams or individually, answer the story-specific questions; keep your answers to 25–75 words for each question.
2. In teams of three to five persons each, or as a whole class, discuss your responses to the critical thinking questions.
3. Prepare a one-page memo report (200–250 words) to your instructor in which you summarize this article. You will find a model one-page report on the Web site (nytimes.swcollege.com).
4. Write an executive summary (200–250 words). As an administrative assistant to a busy executive, you are expected to summarize selected articles and present important points. You will find a model executive summary on the Web site.

5. Summarize this article (100–125 words) for your company's newsletter. You will find a model newsletter article on the Web site.
6. You are a middle-aged employee of a company about to change from a traditional pension plan to a cash-balance plan. Develop a one-page newsletter, persuading employees to fight back.
7. You are the corporate finance officer for a company about to change from a traditional pension plan to a cash-balance pension plan. Develop a one-page newsletter, persuading employees to accept this plan.

BUILDING RESEARCH SKILLS

1. Review the Age Discrimination in Employment Act (http://www.law.cornell.edu. uscode/29/621.html). Summarize the act and explain how it could be applied to the IBM case. Present the information in a paper (800–1,000 words).
2. Individually or in teams, research and compare the retirement plans of three publicly traded companies. Do any of their plans offer a cash-balance plan? Who is eligible? What is the estimated cost to the company? Your instructor may ask you to submit a three- to five-page essay, post a Web page or report your results in a five-minute presentation, along with a letter of transmittal explaining your findings.
3. Individually or in teams, develop an equitable pension plan. What are the plan's eligibility requirements? Costs? Proposed benefits to the employee? Costs to the corporation? Financial justification? Your instructor may ask you to submit a three- to five-page essay, post a Web page or report your results in a five-minute presentation, along with a letter of transmittal explaining your findings.
4. Using at least three other references (e.g., books, research-journal articles, newspaper or magazine stories or credible Web sites), write an 800- to 1,000-word essay that addresses two of the critical thinking questions offered earlier. Assume that your essay will be used as an internal reference for a financial institution's investment guidelines.
5. Using at least three other references (e.g., books, research-journal articles, newspaper or magazine stories or credible Web sites), post an 800- to 1,000-word Web page that addresses at least two of the earlier critical thinking questions. Assume that your page will be posted in the investment section of a corporate intranet.

Personal Finance and Investment Management

PREVIEW

Money, money, money. This chapter examines how individuals can earn it, keep it and invest it to make it grow.

In "Betting the Farm On the Virtual Store," Roy Furchgott examines the trials and tribulations that electronic entrepreneurs face in the burgeoning field of online auctions. As his story illustrates, digital auctioneers balance potentially high profits and the capacity to stay open for business 24 hours a day against long hours at the computer, Web-site crashes, irate customers and the tedium of wrapping and sending countless packages.

Assuming that one profits from online auctioneering, Richard A. Oppel Jr.'s "The Index Monster in Your Closet," examines what may happen with investing your hard-earned profits into an indexed mutual fund. Closet indexing, when fund managers essentially mimic a benchmark stock market index, is an increasingly common and expensive trend among mutual funds.

Eliminating unnecessary and frivolous expenses, such as paying a mutual fund manager for services not rendered, is the underlying philosophy behind Rick Marin's article, "Confessions of a Frugal Spendthrift." In this light-hearted story, Marin reports his personal experiences as he subjects himself to a hard-nosed audit of his sometimes silly and sometimes serious expenditures.

Source: Christine M. Thompson/CyberTimes

Betting the Farm On the Virtual Store
More People Try to Make a Living Through Web Auctions

By Roy Furchgott

For eight years, Fred Parks says, he sold all manner of antiques and collectibles, "everything but tube socks and T-shirts," from a series of stores in downtown Baltimore. About a year ago, he closed his latest store, but he didn't go out of business. He took his expertise in ceramics—Art Nouveau, Art Deco and Arts and Crafts styles—to Ebay, the largest of the online auction sites.

Now working from home and a studio that he rents for $100 a month, he has lowered his expenses, he says, and increased his prices and profits. "If I opened a store, I might have 35 people on a good day," he said. "I get thousands in my virtual store."

More and more people are making a living from online auctions, often closing their brick-and-mortar stores or quitting jobs to vend bric-a-brac electronically at auctions like the ones at Ebay (www.ebay.com), Amazon.com (www.amazon.com) and Yahoo (www.yahoo.com). According to a report issued in March by Forrester Research, a consulting company that tracks E-commerce, spending on auction sites will grow from $1 billion in 1998 to an estimated $2.3 billion this year. While none of the auction sites knows how many people have turned electronic auctions into full-time jobs, Ebay estimates that it has about 10,000 "power sellers," who sell merchandise for $2,000 to $25,000 or more each month.

Parks said he had no regrets about going virtual. "I at this point have no interest in ever having a store again," he said. "Why would I?"

Why? Well, there are the long hours at the computer, and the tedium of wrapping and sending countless packages. Sometimes the auction sites crash, suspending business for days and putting a crimp in the cash flow. And there are the prickly customers who think nothing of firing off rude e-mail tirades. But for Parks and others, the increased profits and ability to open for business at any hour are ample compensation for the drawbacks of Web auctions.

The Forrester Research study projects that by 2003, auction sites will account for $6.4 billion in spending.

As more store owners get a taste of selling online, more stores will close, analysts predict. Michael May, a digital commerce analyst for Jupiter Communications, a research firm in Boston, explained: "They are Main Street, mom-and-pop-type stores that realize they are selling a far greater percentage of their inventory through sites like Ebay, and they can't justify paying rent anymore."

For instance, take Mike Baker, who had averaged $30,000 to $40,000 in revenue a year selling baseball cards and photographs from his store in Springdale, Arkansas. Now he makes bulk purchases of movie star photos and art prints to sell in online auctions, and he reports that his gross revenue is in six figures.

Baker said he had been initially startled by the effectiveness of auction sales two years ago when he posted some Marilyn Monroe photos that were readily available from other sources. "If I got $6 back, I broke even; if I sold them for $12, I did good," he said. They sold for $36.10 each. (Baker has since self-published a book, *Strike it Rich on Ebay*.)

Or take Chris Gwynn, who quit his job as a marketing analyst with the Yankee Group in Boston to sell refrigerator magnets on line. He has now branched out to auctioning new action figures and has created his own site (actionfigureauctions.com) to sell them.

Gwynn makes less money than he did as an analyst. "But within a year," he said, "I should be doing a lot better than I was."

Auction sites have made it fairly simple for people to hang out a shingle because they require sellers to do little more than enter information in a series of text boxes. That has made it possible for even the computer-phobic to become involved in E-commerce.

"I was scared of it and I thought I was too old to learn," said Claudia Bennett, an antiques dealer in Vernon, Texas. Ms. Bennett, who is 52, is now designing her own Web page, and she says she does not regret closing her 14,000-square-foot store or quitting her job at the post office to underwrite her antiques operation. "Now for the first time, I am making money at it," she said.

While anyone can sell online, not just anyone can make a living at it. "It's not as easy as saying, 'I am an E-merchant,' " said Parks, who bought a $1,200 digital camera, lights and a booth to make his ceramics and other wares look appealing online. "A bad photograph will not make you money."

Even though successful, full-time auction entrepreneurs set their own hours, they say the job is extremely demanding. One such Web merchant, Lisa Harrington, said she had owned a tropical fish store in Houston that went bankrupt. But six years after the bankruptcy, she was drawn into Ebay when she helped a friend who was struggling with an online business. She struck out on her own in June 1998, and in the year that followed, she said, she took in $250,000, selling everything from electronics to motorized self-scooping cat litter boxes.

To generate that kind of income, Mrs. Harrington signs on at 8:30 A.M. on workdays and does not sign off until 2 A.M., taking only an hour on some days to watch a soap opera. She takes only Fridays and Mondays off. "They are dead," she said.

On a typical workday, she handles about 600 e-mail messages, monitors 20 auctions and packages about 20 items for shipping. She also has to scare up fresh stock over the phone and online.

Although customers pay for shipping fees—and Mrs. Harrington confides that she sometimes makes a small profit on the shipping charges—there are other costs that new sellers tend to overlook, like the fees charged by auction sites, usually a percentage of the selling price. Mrs. Harrington said that she paid an average of $2,000 a month to Ebay alone. She also uses sites like Utrade, Ubid, Haggle and 321Gone.

Baker also puts in long hours selling his celebrity photos and art prints. "I start at 6 every morning," he said. "I work until 6. Then I take a break. Then I go back up around 10."

Alan Hunter, who auctions sports and political memorabilia online, said he put in eight hours a day photographing items, writing descriptions, uploading information onto the day's auction sites, answering e-mail and packing up items to be mailed out. "But that doesn't include the time you spend hunting this stuff up," he said. "The toughest part is that you have a commitment to it every single day."

Those who are not willing to put in long hours may get involved in too few auctions to really make money. Even worse, they may be slow to respond to customers, which can result in the posting of complaints referred to as dreaded "negative feedback."

When a transaction is completed, the seller and buyer can write a short message commenting on it. Such feedback is available for all to see, and it works as a self-policing mechanism, warning people away from buyers or sellers who other people think are dishonest.

The problem for someone selling goods at a lot of auctions is that it is easy to accrue negative comments. The more customers a seller has, the greater the chances that some of them will be slow to pay or hard to satisfy. If a seller posts a complaint about a buyer, the buyer may retaliate. "And before you know it," Hunter said, "you have 20 negative feedbacks." The alternative is for a seller to grin and bear it when dealing with a testy buyer—a frequent occurrence.

Sellers often try to increase profits a few percentage points by avoiding auction site fees. For instance, there is no rule against a seller getting in touch with auction losers to make separate deals if the seller has multiple copies of an item.

Arlen Miller, who quit his job at Planet Hollywood in Orlando two years ago to deal full time online in Disney collectibles, said: "I'll look at Ebay stuff, and if I have the same item on my list, I'll go back when the auction is over. You can go in and look at all of the bidders. If it went for $50, and I have it for $30, I'll send a note."

But Miller draws an ethical line. "I would never step on someone's toes by doing that before their auction is over."

The auction game is outgrowing the boundaries of Ebay, Amazon and Yahoo. The Forrester study predicted that the future of online auctions would be in sales of new retail products sold by companies, often on their own sites, rather than by individuals.

"Over time, consumers will prefer buying from businesses rather than individuals since businesses are more accountable and offer first-run merchandise," the report said. A check using Yahoo's search engine turned up a list of close to 200 auction sites, including head-to-head Ebay competitors as well as specialty sites like Justbeads.com, which auctions beads, and Floorspace.com, which auctions industrial machinery.

Off-the-shelf auction software makes it possible for individuals and small businesses to set up their own auction sites. "Auction software costs about $5,000," said Gwynn, the refrigerator magnet magnate who sells his action figures on his own site. "The server is a few hundred dollars a month."

Gwynn does not allow other people to sell on his site. If he had set up the site that way, he said, he would have been competing against Ebay; that, he added, would be a losing proposition.

In an early test of his sales plan, Gwynn said, he auctioned 96 Austin Powers figures, which sell at retail for about $11, in a week. He sold many of them in the $20 range, and some for as much as $38. "They were popular that week, and they were hard to get," he said.

Not all the figures have flown off the shelves. Gwynn has found it difficult to sell everything from Barbie to "Star Wars" figures on a single site. So he will soon specialize even more. He plans to set up auction sites that are organized to reflect the way collectors collect: by manufacturer. That will make it easier to reach collectors looking for specific toys through online bulletin boards and newsletters, he said.

While the online auction entrepreneurs do a lot of selling, they do little buying on line. "I never have really been able to buy on Ebay to re-sell and make a profit on it," said Baker, the print seller.

In fact, some sellers worry about what Ebay and other sites will mean for their sources for items, like garage sales, if everyone is selling everything, including the kitchen sink, online.

So far those fears have proved to be unfounded. The number of yard sales each weekend proves that people still need to clean out their attics—and that most of them still do it the off-line way, especially if they don't own a digital camera.

The New York Times, September 9, 1999
http://www.nytimes.com/library/tech/99/09/circuits/articles/09ebay.html

CRITICAL THINKING QUESTIONS

1. Are Web auctions a passing fad? Why, or why not?
2. Would you advise someone to go into the Web auction business? Why, or why not?
3. What are the advantages and disadvantages of going into the Web auction business?
4. Will Web auctions be the death of "brick and mortar" retail stores? Explain.

5. What are the possible expenses and revenues at Web auction sites?
6. What are effective Web auction strategies for the buyer? For the seller?

STORY-SPECIFIC QUESTIONS

1. According to a report issued in March by Forrester Research, a consulting company that tracks E-commerce, consumer spending at auction sites grew how much from 1998 to 1999? What about by 2003?
2. The story mentions what three popular auction sites?
3. What did Forrester predict about the future of online auctions?
4. What is a typical workday for Harrington?

SHORT APPLICATION ASSIGNMENTS

1. In teams or individually, answer the story-specific questions; keep your answers to 25–75 words for each question.
2. In teams of three to five persons each, or as a whole class, discuss your responses to the critical thinking questions.
3. Prepare a one-page memo report (200–250 words) to your instructor in which you summarize this article. You will find a model one-page report on the Web site (nytimes.swcollege.com).
4. Write an executive summary (200–250 words). As an administrative assistant to a busy executive, you are expected to summarize selected articles and present important points. You will find a model executive summary on the Web site.
5. Summarize this article (100–125 words) for your company's newsletter. You will find a model newsletter article on the Web site.
6. Read "Auction Sales Strategies" (http://www.nytimes.com/library/tech/99/09/circuits/articles/09ebay-tips.html), which is linked to this article. Your instructor may ask you to present your findings in an oral report or submit a 150- to 200-word summary.

BUILDING RESEARCH SKILLS

1. Individually or in teams, explore the eBay (http://www.ebay.com), Yahoo (http://auction.yahoo.com) and Amazon (http://auction.amazon.com) auction sites for a specific product. How easy is the site to navigate? Did you find the product? Were the bid prices similar? Your instructor may assign you a product or you may choose one. Your instructor may also ask you to submit a three- to five-page essay, post a Web page or report your results in a five-minute presentation, along with a letter of transmittal explaining your findings.
2. Individually or in teams, auction an item on the eBay (http://www.ebay.com), Yahoo (http://auction.yahoo.com) or Amazon (http://auction.amazon.com) auction sites. Did your item sell? Was the process easy? What would you do differently the next time? Your instructor may also ask you to submit a three- to five-page essay, post a Web page or report your results in a five-minute presentation, along with a letter of transmittal explaining your findings.

3. Using at least three other references (e.g., books, research-journal articles, news-paper or magazine stories or credible Web sites), write an 800- to 1,000-word essay that addresses two of the critical thinking questions offered earlier. Assume that your essay will be used as an internal reference for a financial institution's investment guidelines.
4. Using at least three other references (e.g., books, research-journal articles, news-paper or magazine stories or credible Web sites), post an 800- to 1,000-word Web page that addresses at least two of the earlier critical thinking questions. Assume that your page will be posted in the investment section of a corporate intranet.

The Index Monster in Your Closet

By Richard A. Oppel Jr.

Microsoft. General Electric. IBM. Wal-Mart Stores. Cisco Systems. These are the companies that have led this decade's bull market. The next time a shareholder report for your stock mutual fund comes in the mail, take a look at its top holdings: You may find a lot of these big names.

If your fund has held such stocks for a long time, chances are that it has beaten most other funds in performance. And that may lead you to believe that you have lucked into a superior fund manager.

But not everyone may come to that conclusion. Some will tell you that instead, you are actually a victim of an increasingly common and expensive trend toward "closet indexing," in which mutual fund managers essentially mimic a benchmark index. And it is a practice that provokes some strong responses.

"A big rip-off," said Robert Sanborn, who manages the Oakmark Fund.

John C. Bogle, the founder of the Vanguard Group, calls the practice "horrendous."

Closet indexing works like this: A fund manager invests most of a fund's assets in stocks that comprise the bulk of a particular index. The manager invests the rest in other stocks—or to double up on a few from the index. Despite the lack of significant stock-picking, the fund still charges fees that are 3 to 10 times as high as those of a basic index fund, which simply tracks a benchmark.

Though shareholders pay a lot extra for such "active management," the fund, over time, is unlikely to beat the index by any significant margin. More likely, it will lag behind it—largely because of the higher fees. And it will bring higher taxes, because it trades stocks more often. That is not good for investors.

But because so much of the actively managed fund is tied to an index, it will probably not trail the benchmark by much, thus avoiding the huge underperformance—say 10 percent or more—that prompts investors to withdraw their money. That is good news for the fund company.

Closet indexing is not new. But new figures crunched by Morningstar Inc., the Chicago financial publisher, show just how strong the trend has become.

To get your arms around the idea, it helps to understand a measure called "R-squared," which gauges the correlation between a fund and whatever index—usually the Standard & Poor's 500-stock index—it is measured against. If a fund has an R-squared of, say, 90, that means that 90 percent of the fund's movement can be explained by movements in the component stocks of the index.

Morningstar found that for the three years ended in August, the R-squared of the average actively managed United States stock fund was more than 74, up from 58 in the three years ended in December 1994.

And among large-capitalization funds—where stock fund investors keep $2 out of every $3—the average offering had an R-squared of more than 86, up from 71. Over all, the numbers mean that more and more of the return of United States stock funds is tied to changes in the S&P 500.

In fact, five years ago, only one in 12 large-cap funds had an R-squared of 90 or higher; that compares with two out of five today. As of August, the percentage of such funds had declined somewhat from year-end 1998, but researchers say that there is a strong seasonal factor to the R-squared phenomenon, with managers making their portfolios more like those of their indexes as the year comes to a close.

Even so, one of every seven large-cap funds—including a number of the biggest funds in the country—still score 95 or higher. Most of these are virtually indexed portfolios but with far higher expenses than an index fund, Bogle said.

"If it looks like a duck, walks like a duck, quacks like a duck, it's probably a duck," Bogle said. "You're paying a ton more, and you're getting more turnover, which is a horrible tax expense, and you're getting fees that are extremely difficult to justify."

Of course, you might expect Bogle to cry foul, because it is his company's flagship offering—the Vanguard Index 500 fund—that is the subject of the rampant imitation.

The mimicry springs from a number of factors, according to fund managers, executives and recruiters.

Fund companies used to be far more willing to tolerate swings in performance, allowing managers to act on their convictions. Now, more fund families are single-mindedly focused on the bottom line—and have found that hewing closely to a predictable investing style is a good way to attract new customers and to retain old ones.

And in corporate America, the executives who choose funds for their employees' 401(k) plans, which now account for one-third to one-half of fund sales at many larger fund families, put a high premium on performance that is consistent with popular benchmarks. Such consistency means that corporate officers, often human resources executives, can avoid the embarrassment of trying to explain why the large-cap growth fund they selected for the 401(k) is badly trailing the overall market.

But individual investors have helped to spur the development, too. Increasingly, they want to make their own decisions on market timing and asset allocation, and so resent managers who take these decisions out of their hands. They don't want to wake up and find, for example, that their large-cap equity fund has put its assets into cash, bonds or small stocks.

At the same time, many fund managers have stopped swinging for the fences, because they know the penalties for severely underperforming an index are now much greater than the rewards for strongly outperforming it. Nor does it help that the S&P 500 has clobbered most funds the last half-dozen years.

The compensation packages of fund managers also feed the trend toward closet indexing, executive recruiters and industry officials say. A recent survey found that the average manager of a big U.S. stock fund makes most of his money through bonuses. Looking at all portfolio managers, the survey found that their firm's bottom-line performance matters almost as much as their own stock-picking records in figuring bonuses.

Fund industry officials and recruiters say pay packages are most often structured in ways that encourage managers to beat their peers but discourage them from taking the risks necessary to significantly outperform their benchmarks. For instance, a manager might get a much higher bonus for finishing in the top 20 percent of his peer group, but not much more for finishing in the top few percent.

Finally, many funds have become so big and unwieldy that it has become more difficult to buy and sell large stakes in companies, or to make big sector bets that can make substantial differences in performance. Indeed, the difficulty of managing large pools of money actively has long been an argument in favor of indexing.

What does all this signify for investors? In short, it means that they may be paying for active management but actually getting something that may closely resemble an index fund but has little chance of beating one.

Indeed, some industry analysts say that the time has long passed when investors could simply choose between an index fund and one that sought to beat the market through smart stock-picking. Now, if they pick the actively managed route, they must choose between funds that hang close to the index or those that theoretically could significantly outperform it—or, of course, lag behind it by a wide margin.

Consider the performance of the five largest actively managed stock funds with R-squareds of 95 or higher for the three years ended August 31. They returned 21 percent to 26.9 percent annually over that period. Adjusted for the taxes an investor would have paid on dividends and capital gains distributions, the five returned 18 percent to 24.6 percent, according to Morningstar.

Index funds did better than any of those, with Vanguard's Index 500, the largest S&P 500 index fund, returning 28.5 percent (27.5 percent, adjusted for taxes).

And of the 80 largest actively managed funds with scores of 95 or higher for the three years, only three—Vanguard Growth and Income, Goldman Sachs Capital Growth class A and Pioneer class A, beat the index fund—but not by much. And none were able to do so on a tax-adjusted basis. These 80 funds control nearly $400 billion of investors' money.

After repeatedly trailing the S&P 500 in recent years, active managers have a shot at outperforming the index in 1999. But that doesn't mean that funds with high R-squareds will necessarily do better.

For the first three quarters this year, the performance of the five largest funds with R-squareds of at least 95 ranged from a 0.3 percent loss to a 5 percent gain, compared with a gain of 5.4 percent for the S&P 500.

Does all this mean that investors should opt for a fund simply because its performance is unlikely to resemble S&P 500 returns? Of course not. By and large, you would have been better off in a closet index fund during the last few years than one that truly sought to beat the market—as most of those failed miserably in that goal. You might say closet indexing is the next best thing to an actual index fund.

But the issue is more complicated than that. Many investors subscribe to the widely held notion that portfolios should be divided among indexed and actively managed funds, as a way to reduce risk. To avoid costly duplication, however, they may want to stay away from keeping a combination of index funds and actively managed funds with high R-squared numbers.

Still, the list of large funds with low R-squareds has lately read like the roster of an underachievers' club. Among them are some lauded value and growth funds, that despite strong long-term records, have endured extraordinary rough patches over the last few years.

They include the Mutual Series funds, the Brandywine Fund, Vanguard Windsor, C.G.M. Capital Development, Sequoia Fund and Sanborn's Oakmark Fund, to name a few.

That's not to say none have succeeded, even in the late '90s, when just a very small group of stocks have led the S&P 500 higher. Most notable, perhaps, are the funds of Janus Capital, several of which have easily beaten the S&P 500 over the last few years. As a result, Janus has attracted $22 billion in new cash into its funds in the first eight months of the year, ranking it number two in terms of cash flow among fund families, after Vanguard.

The largest of Janus' family, the $32 billion Janus Fund, has a three-year R-squared of 78, with top holdings as of July 31 that include American Express, Charles Schwab, Cisco Systems, Comcast and Enron. The second-largest, Janus 20, scored a 68 and lately has made its biggest bets on America Online, American International Group, Cisco, Dell Computer and GE. (While all of these stocks are in the S&P 500, their weightings in the funds are far different than they are in the index.)

The lesson is that big rewards still remain for managers who can shoot the lights out. But the unfaithful flow of investor cash punishes those who try and fail.

Witness Sanborn of Oakmark, a standout performer in the early 90s. His huge bets on companies like First U.S.A. and Liberty Media paid off with a 35 percent annual return during the three years after its inception in August 1991, compared with about 10 percent for the S&P 500. But the last three years have been a different story: Oakmark has returned 12.9 percent annualized for the three years through September 30, or less than half the index's performance.

As a result, in the last year, investors have pulled more than $2 billion out of his fund, which now has $5.6 billion in assets, according to AMG Data Services.

"I feel bad about it," Sanborn said, "but I wouldn't necessarily do anything different." That is seen in his recent stock picks, which have included no technology, energy or utilities stocks—sectors that comprise more than a third of the S&P 500. But he does have big stakes in companies with strong consumer franchises like Philip Morris, H&R Block, Nike, Dun & Bradstreet, Knight Ridder, Mattel and Black & Decker.

Sanborn is even willing to suggest that some investors may be better off indexing. "Most fund investors are grossly overdiversified. They should sell everything and have a portfolio of index funds, or truly try to outperform," he said, adding that "having a guy manage a closet index fund, charging active fees, is a very poor value."

But that kind of thinking is harder to find at many fund companies. That can be attributed in part to the "style police"—fund company executives, fund analysts, consultants, customers, journalists and other assorted critics who lambaste those fund managers who suffer poor performance because they stray from the sort of stocks that people expect them to hold.

"Fund managers are under greater pressure to toe the line," said Nancy Miller, director of client services at the Mark Elzweig Co., a New York investment management executive search firm. "They will get slapped down for not staying within their discipline, with customers and 401(k) plans breathing down their neck. They can't afford to be cowboys any more."

One oft-cited example of this kind of pressure is the case of Jeffrey N. Vinik, the former Magellan manager, who left Fidelity in 1996 after putting 35 percent of the fund's assets into cash and bonds, thus missing out on continued strong performance in the stock market. (At the time, Vinik said he was "absolutely not" asked to leave and that Fidelity's chairman, Edward C. Johnson III, had recently given him a vote of confidence.)

Another example is Brandywine's Foster S. Friess, who went heavily into cash in early 1998 while the market continued to rise, then plowed his money back into stocks later in the year, a few months before the market suffered a 20 percent decline—moves that prompted investors to pull more than $3 billion from the fund that year, according to AMG.

Vinik's market-timing skills have since been revalidated—he now runs a top-performing hedge fund, Vinik Asset Management in Boston—while Brandywine is beating the S&P 500 by 12.9 percentage points this year through Wednesday.

Fidelity, after seeing poor performance at a number of its big funds, began emphasizing quarterly audits of managers in 1997, when Robert C. Pozen was appointed to oversee Fidelity's fund family. Some analysts say these audits, called "quarterly fund reviews," may lessen the odds that a big Fidelity fund will ever make another Vinik-style sector bet or market call.

The reviews examine how a manager performs compared with his peers and benchmark. Poor returns can thus be explained by looking at what poorly performing stocks and sectors they owned—or what rising stocks and sectors they did not own.

Fidelity says the reviews do not encourage closet indexing, although data from Morningstar suggest that most of Fidelity's biggest funds have not recently strayed far from the S&P. 500. In fact, eight of Fidelity's 11 largest actively managed funds have three-year R-squareds of 94 or higher.

A number of big Fidelity funds have had "correlation creep" with regard to the S&P 500, said Jim Lowell, editor of *Fidelity Investor*, an independent newsletter based in Potomac, Maryland. But he says that is not because of closet indexing, noting that many large Fidelity funds beat the index last year. Fidelity managers have "recognized that the leadership stocks basically exist within the S&P 500, so it's not too surprising to look at their top 10 holdings and find a lot of familiar names."

Fidelity also uses performance fees, meaning that the amount it charges investors rises or falls depending on whether a fund beats or trails its benchmark. This pay-for-performance is rare in the industry: Lipper Inc. calculates that such fees are used by only 150 of the 12,000 U.S. funds, including Fidelity's.

Fidelity dismisses the notion that it is a closet indexer. A spokeswoman, Anne Crowley, noted that some of Fidelity's biggest funds beat the S&P 500 by a wide margin for the year ended September 30, including the $94 billion Magellan, which topped the index by 8.3 percentage points. With such a difference in performance, Ms. Crowley said, "to say that it's highly correlated with the S&P doesn't seem that relevant."

She also noted that because Fidelity is one of the few fund companies that uses performance fees, it stands to lose or gain hundreds of millions of dollars every year depending on whether its funds beat their benchmark indexes—providing a strong incentive not to closet-index.

But as Morningstar's numbers demonstrate, index mimicry is occurring across the board.

"You've had a change in the fund management industry," said Richard S. Lannamann, who oversees investment management recruiting at Russell Reynolds Associates, an executive search firm based in New York. "People used to trust their money to the fund with the expectation that the fund manager would do what he thought best for shareholders," including raising cash or making big sector or capitalization bets.

"Now most fund management companies are running with the assumption than an investor bought a particular product because they want to be exposed to that asset class, and they don't want a fund manager to time the market and make big bets," Lannamann said. "A lot of value is placed on style consistency and risk control, reflecting the dominance of the pension markets," including 401(k) plans.

Don't look to fund company executives to try to change that anytime soon. Chief executives of investment management companies are roughly twice as likely to be awarded bonuses based on their company's bottom-line performance as on how well their funds perform, according to a recent survey by Russell Reynolds and the Association for Investment Management and Research, a trade group.

You might say investors get what their fund executives are paid for.

The New York Times, October 10, 1999
http://www.nytimes.com/library/financial/sunday/101099mutfund-overview.html

CRITICAL THINKING QUESTIONS

1. Is closet indexing a rip-off? Why, or why not?
2. What are the advantages and disadvantages of investing in an index fund?
3. What are the advantages and disadvantages of an actively managed fund?
4. Would you advise someone to invest in an actively managed or an index fund? Explain.

STORY-SPECIFIC QUESTIONS

1. How does closet indexing work?
2. What is "R squared" and how does it work?
3. According to the story, what five stocks have led the 1990's bull market?
4. Fund industry officials and recruiters say pay packages are most often structured in what ways?
5. What are style police?

SHORT APPLICATION ASSIGNMENTS

1. In teams or individually, answer the story-specific questions; keep your answers to 25–75 words for each question.
2. In teams of three to five persons each, or as a whole class, discuss your responses to the critical thinking questions.
3. Prepare a one-page memo report (200–250 words) to your instructor in which you summarize this article. You will find a model one-page report on the Web site (nytimes.swcollege.com).
4. Write an executive summary (200–250 words). As an administrative assistant to a busy executive, you are expected to summarize selected articles and present important points. You will find a model executive summary on the Web site.
5. Summarize this article (100–125 words) for your company's newsletter. You will find a model newsletter article on the Web site.

BUILDING RESEARCH SKILLS

1. Individually or in teams, explore the Fidelity (http://www.fidelity.com), Vanguard (http://www.vanguard.com) and Janus (http://www.janus.com) Web sites. You may also call their toll free number to research some of these questions. How many index funds does each offer? What has been the performance over the last year of their S&P 500 fund? What are the fees associated with each company's S&P 500 fund? How easy is each site to navigate? Your instructor may ask you to submit a three- to five-page essay, post a Web page or report your results in a five-minute presentation, along with a letter of transmittal explaining your findings.

2. Individually or in teams, read three of the articles listed on *The New York Times on the Web* Mutual Funds Report (http://www.nytimes.com/library/financial/sunday/mutfund-index.html). Your instructor may ask you to submit a three- to five-page essay, post a Web page or report your results in a five-minute presentation, along with a letter of transmittal explaining your findings.

3. Using at least three other references (e.g., books, research-journal articles, newspaper or magazine stories or credible Web sites), write an 800- to 1,000-word essay that addresses two of the critical thinking questions offered earlier. Assume that your essay will be used as an internal reference for a financial institution's investment guidelines.

4. Using at least three other references (e.g., books, research-journal articles, newspaper or magazine stories or credible Web sites), post an 800- to 1,000-word Web page that addresses at least two of the earlier critical thinking questions. Assume that your page will be posted in the investment section of a corporate intranet.

Confessions of a Frugal Spendthrift

By Rick Marin

Frugality has never been my problem. I've always made enough to cover my rent or mortgage. I pay my bills on time. I've never been in serious debt. And yet, compared with my parents, I'm a spendthrift.

I leave lights on in my Manhattan apartment. I'm a sucker for the service economy: trainers, housekeepers, tennis pros. And every time I buy an absurdly expensive suit, pay too much for dinner or spring for an unnecessarily fancy hotel, I feel guilty.

Not guilty enough not to blow $2,000 on a cool '60s-modern credenza, but guilty enough to resolve to be more cost conscious in the future. So I take the subway instead of a cab and think I'm a hero—until the next bout of buyer's remorse.

Clearly, a deeper kind of fiscal self-examination is called for. So I got in touch with the authors of *Invest in Yourself: Six Secrets to a Rich Life* (John Wiley & Sons, 1998) and offered to subject myself to the ultimate humiliation: a frugality audit.

Written by Marc Eisenson, Gerri Detweiler and Nancy Castleman, the book's 328 pages blend self-help of the simple-abundance school with hardcore financial belt-tightening tips and complicated charts. Reading it you become convinced you could become a millionaire by paying an extra $50 a month on your mortgage or by buying used cars.

Who better to cast a cold eye on my platinum card bill? A frightening idea. There are things on those statements I don't even want to admit to myself, much less expose to complete strangers.

We traded e-mails. Eisenson and Ms. Castleman, a happily unmarried couple for 19 years, live together on a farm in Red Hook, New York, and publish a quarterly newsletter called the *Pocket Change Investor*, which they describe as a guide to "living better on less." They wanted me to visit their bucolic paradise of organic vegetables. But I felt that to be appropriately appalled by my decadence, they needed to spring for train fare to Manhattan.

In the meantime, they made a series of requests. Information about my monthly mortgage payment, which was recently doubled by the purchase of a summer house, and my 401(k) situation. Phone and utilities bills. Checkbook. A 1998 tax return.

Ms. Detweiler, for many years the director of a consumer group called Bankcard Holders of America, asked me to keep a "spending diary," accounting for every penny I shelled out over a week. Ms. Castleman and Eisenson wanted me to think not just about money but about quality of life issues.

"We're not financial planners," Ms. Detweiler e-mailed me. "We're more 'life style' planners, geared toward helping you create more of the life you want on any income (not just when your portfolio reaches a certain level and you can 'retire')." She added, "Where are you investing your time and energy well, and where do you seem to fall short? What kinds of changes have you been putting off because of money?"

Hey, I thought but didn't write back, if I had a lot of extra time, I'd be using it. Changes? I'd buy a grotesquely huge house in the Hamptons and spend my days by the pool ordering gimlets from my houseboy!

Defensive? Of course. Anything to avoid thinking too hard about such things.

But the "Invest in Yourself" trio continued bombarding me with subliminal frugality messages.

From Ms. Castleman, re lunch: "Are you by any chance allergic to sunflower seeds?! (I usually use them in my pesto because they're a lot cheaper than pine nuts, and we can't tell the difference.)"

How's anyone supposed to enjoy an overpriced bowl of pasta under this kind pressure?

The lunch date rolled around and the three of them showed up at my apartment with a bowl of sunflower pesto in hand. Eisenson has a long gray beard and the look of someone who checked out of the rat race—in his case, an electrical contracting business—a long time ago.

Remember Natural, R. Crumb's aging cartoon hippie? That's Eisenson, only, it turns out, with a sense of humor and a savant's skill at crunching numbers in his head. Ms. Castleman is wearing the same sandals she wore to Woodstock in 1969. Literally. Ms. Detweiler, who is about 20 years younger than her co-authors, lives outside Washington, D.C., wore a suit and evinced a little less of the converts' zeal than her collaborators.

As we sat down to salad from Ms. Castleman and Eisenson's Red Hook herb garden—served in a bowl purchased for $1 in 1970—I asked how long it took to grow the tomato we were eating.

"About 1,000 hours of labor," Eisenson said. "That's a $50 tomato."

Which was why I mentioned it. If your time is worth X dollars an hour, is it worth spending the time for less than that amount of money in savings? Eisenson offered a sort of zen reply: "There are times when our time should be worth nothing."

I wasn't going to win that argument, so I told them I needed a car. I've never minded not having one, but with the new house, it seemed to be a necessity. There comes a time in every man's life—like at age 37—when he should stop having to borrow his girlfriend's parents' Land Rover.

They scoffed at the notion of leasing. "Like buying your grandfather a rented tuxedo and burying it," Ms. Detweiler said. Eisenson contended that "most millionaires drive used cars."

Then they started with the scare tactics, presumably based on a careful scrub of my financials. "If you bought a car, you could be really tight," Ms. Detweiler said. "It wouldn't take much to upset the apple cart," Ms. Castleman added darkly.

OK, forget the car. I wanted to get back to the stuff I misspend money on right now, not hypothetical future squanderings. First, I demanded a kitchen inspection. My bottle of Pellegrino was the first subject of ridicule—something wrong with New York City tap water?—then a box of funghi porcini in the cupboard. "I can go out into the woods and pick these," Eisenson said.

Ms. Castleman moved on to my air conditioner, set at a refreshing 65 degrees. "It's nice out!" she scolded.

After our meeting, I was inundated with e-mails from Red Hook alerting me to the 23 percent savings I could enjoy on my electric bill if I turned the air-conditioning up to 72 degrees, 44 percent if I went up to 78 degrees. Sure. I could probably *make* money on the deal if I pushed the thing up to 85 degrees, but I might die of heat prostration.

After hearing that I pay bills the day they arrive, take the subway to work, eat in more than out, they looked disappointed.

"You're much too frugal," Eisenson said.

I knew better. I've always spent too much money on clothes. When I was in high school, my mother used to mock my vast collection of shirts. So I compared notes with Eisenson on our polo shirts: my neo-retro rayon J. Crew that has to be dry-cleaned, $65; his secondhand Gap, five cents.

"You paid $65, but really it cost you $100," he pointed out.

Calculating the "real" cost in earned income is one of the book's simplest and most useful suggestions. Always factor in what taxes take out—in my case, around 30 percent. At this rate, to pay for a $14,000 car you have to make $20,000. Now figure out how long it takes you to make that $20,000. Sobering.

What makes the authors nuts, on the tax front, is the idea that you should spend money to get a deduction. "Every dollar you spend in the hope of saving 30 cents is costing you 70 cents," Eisenson said.

Still desperate to prove my profligacy, I handed over my latest Visa statement. They studied it as if it were some ancient parchment, full of cryptic words and incomprehensible numerals.

"What's Mikimoto?" Ms. Castleman asked, her eyes widening at the accompanying charge.

It's a jewelry store, I mumbled tentatively. Anniversary earrings.

Eisenson offered an alternative "gifting" philosophy: "Take over a chore your mate hates and let that be the present."

That was when I realized we were living in different worlds: theirs and the real world of my girlfriend, who requires baubles that can be either shown off or exchanged.

I bid my guests farewell with promises to send them more complete financial documentation of my paycheck-to-paycheck existence and to keep a spending diary for Ms. Detweiler to review.

I started the week of June 28:

Monday: Forget completely.

Tuesday: Subway ($1.50), oatmeal from company cafeteria (85 cents), cafeteria lunch ($6.60), "American Pie" (free press screening), wine for a friend's sendoff ($12.98). Total: $21.93.

Wednesday: More of the same, with some cabs, drugstore products and $27.85 worth of developed pictures thrown in. Total: $77.80.

Thursday: Host Canada Day party ($79.87 for beer and bacon and maple syrup), my housekeeper ($60), plus a bunch of other stuff, like two pairs of Adidas running shoes ($119). Total: $295.22.

Friday: Housekeeper again, for post-party cleanup ($20), stamps at Mailboxes Etc. ($6.90), CD holder from The Wiz ($8.62), gas (20.09), and—the clincher—*returned* stuff to Bed, Bath and Beyond (–$37.87). Total: $38.99.

The lesson of Ms. Detweiler's exercise, which even she agrees is incredibly tedious, is to show you what you think you spend money on versus what you actually spend money on. I think you're supposed to be surprised at where it all goes. I had the opposite reaction. I was amazed at how little I spend and resolved to live a little better from now on. That 85 cents for oatmeal seemed sadly Dickensian.

A few weeks later, I got an e-mail from Eisenson and Ms. Castleman breaking down some savings options. Dump the health club, to which I hardly ever go (saving $1,000 a year). Mow my own lawn ($2,340 a year). Buy cheaper and fewer clothes ($600). Raise the temperature (Con Ed wouldn't give them figures on that one). Buy cheaper wine ($520).

Each dollar amount was accompanied by a "what you'd have to earn" amount: $1,538 for the health club, $3,600 for the lawn guy. How they arrived at some of these numbers I'm not entirely sure, but I got the point.

I could be more frugal.

It made me think about my late father, who considered my mother a reckless spender, even though she was known as the thrifty one among her friends. They both came from comfortable upper middle-class backgrounds. But she had lived through the Depression, in Canada, and he through the Spanish Civil War.

Both had seen that it was possible to have everything taken away in a trice and I always figured that was why they saved all those bits of old string. He would do things like measure the amount of water in the kettle before boiling it.

My mother still mails me back uncanceled American stamps from Canada, so that I can re-use them. They litter my apartment, like tiny rebukes to my wasteful ways, until I finally get around to soaking them off the old envelope paper and gluing them on a new one.

NANCY'S PESTO

From www.investinyourself.com

Time: 10–15 minutes

20–25 cloves (5 heaping tablespoons) chopped garlic
½ cup sunflower seeds
2 tablespoons vegetable oil
1 tablespoon honey (optional)
1 cup water
6 cups well-packed basil leaves (more or less).

1. Traditional recipes have you use a mortar to pound, or pestare, the ingredients—thus the name of the dish. It goes a lot faster with a food processor or blender.
2. Either way, combine the garlic and sunflower seeds with the oil and honey, and a little of the water. Gradually add the rest of the water.
3. the basil, 2 cups at a time. Process until everything is well blended.

Yield: 4 cups of pesto.

A couple of weekends ago I went to my first warehouse club, a hangar-sized temple to frugality called B.J.'s on Long Island. On the way in I silently disdained all the people rolling giant flatbed carts piled high with toilet paper and frozen swedish meatballs toward the 800-items-or-less cash register. On the way out, I had filled two of those carts myself. Grand total: $531.47. But the important thing was how much I *saved*.

By substituting sunflower seeds for pine nuts, Nancy Castleman's pesto recipe may offend culinary purists. But for the frugal gourmet, it is one more way to save.

Ms. Castleman and her co-author and companion, Marc Eisenson, figure they consume a pint of sunflower pesto weekly, and thus 6.8 pounds of sunflower seeds a year. At the health-food store where they shop in Rhinebeck, New York, the seeds cost 99 cents a pound, versus $10 a pound for pine nuts. So their annual saving, on a nut-for-nut basis, is $61.27 a year.

By Ms. Castleman's calculations, the pine nut premium would cost an extra $94.25 in pretax dollars. But opting for sunflower seeds and investing the savings for 25 years at an average 8 percent return would yield $4,855.78—an impressive harvest.

The New York Times, August 15, 1999

http://www.nytimes.com/library/financial/sunday/081599personal-perfin.html

CRITICAL THINKING QUESTIONS

1. Are you a spendthrift? Explain.
2. Is a "frugality audit" a good idea? Why, or why not?
3. What is the difference between life-style planning and financial planning?
4. Are the frugal ideas raised by this story eccentric? Why, or why not?
5. Is keeping a spending diary a good idea? Why, or why not?

STORY-SPECIFIC QUESTIONS

1. How much could the author save by changing the thermostat for air conditioning?
2. How does one calculate the "real cost" in earned income?
3. Why does Eisenson object to spending money to get a tax deductions?
4. What is Eisenson's alternative gifting philosophy?

SHORT APPLICATION ASSIGNMENTS

1. In teams or individually, answer the story-specific questions; keep your answers to 25–75 words for each question.
2. In teams of three to five persons each, or as a whole class, discuss your responses to the critical thinking questions.
3. Prepare a one-page memo report (200–250 words) to your instructor in which you summarize this article. You will find a model one-page report on the Web site (nytimes.swcollege.com).
4. Write an executive summary (200–250 words). As an administrative assistant to a busy executive, you are expected to summarize selected articles and present important points. You will find a model executive summary on the Web site.
5. Summarize this article (100–125 words) for your company's newsletter. You will find a model newsletter article on the Web site.
6. Read the complementary story, "Six Steps to Monetary and Spiritual Rewards" (http://www.nytimes.com/library/financial/sunday/081599personal-perfin-tips.html). Apply these six steps to your personal finance. Your instructor may ask you to present your findings in an oral report or submit a 150- to 200-word summary.

BUILDING RESEARCH SKILLS

1. Obtain a copy and read *Invest in Yourself: Six Secrets to a Rich Life* by Marc Eisenson, Gerri Detweiler, Nancy Castleman. Write an overview (800–1,000 words) of its central thesis.
2. Keep a spending diary for a week. What did you spend money on versus what you actually thought you spent money on? Your instructor may ask you to submit a three- to five-page essay, post a Web page or report your results in a five-minute presentation, along with a letter of transmittal explaining your findings.
3. Using at least three other references (e.g., books, research-journal articles, newspaper or magazine stories or credible Web sites), write an 800- to 1,000-word essay

that addresses two of the critical thinking questions offered earlier. Assume that your essay will be used as an internal reference for a financial institution's investment guidelines.

4. Using at least three other references (e.g., books, research-journal articles, newspaper or magazine stories or credible Web sites), post an 800- to 1,000-word Web page that addresses at least two of the earlier critical thinking questions. Assume that your page will be posted in the investment section of a corporate intranet.

Finance Today

PREVIEW

Technology and globalization are changing today's financial world. These tandem trends are accelerating the pace and broadening the implications of global financial activity. They also are adding a digital dimension to criminal activities.

Leslie Eaton, along with David Barboza and Diana B. Henriques, describes the underbelly of Wall Street in "Penny-Stock Fraud Is Billion-Dollar Game." As they explain, Wall Street's dark side "is a place of low-priced stocks and high-priced dreams, of swindlers and touts who prey on average people trying to grab the brass ring in the greatest bull market in American history."

Just as penny stocks are difficult to control and regulate at the micro-level, an individual country's financial systems are difficult to control and regulate at the macro-level. Louis Uchitelle's article "Crash Course: Just What's Driving the Crisis in Emerging Markets?" reports on the efforts to frame the debate and find cures to the global financial crisis that began in Southeast Asia and rapidly spread to other developing countries.

Two countries, the United States and Russia, are at center stage in the crime of money laundering. In "Banking 101: The Smaller the Fry, the Hotter the Pan," Timothy L. O'Brien explores how billions of dollars from Russia zipped through a handful of accounts at the Bank of New York for almost two years without anyone taking notice.

Source: Christine M. Thompson/CyberTimes

Penny-Stock Fraud Is Billion-Dollar Game

By Leslie Eaton, with David Barboza and Diana B. Henriques

Most Americans may not know it, but there are really two Wall Streets.

One is the Wall Street of the New York Stock Exchange closing bell, of brash stockbrokers and hair-trigger traders, of big deals and big fortunes, of Microsoft and mutual funds.

But in the crooked alleys of Lower Manhattan flourishes another Wall Street. This is a world of low-priced stocks and high-priced dreams, of grimy offices and sham companies, of swindlers and touts who prey on average people trying to grab the brass ring in the greatest bull market in American history.

Like the world of organized crime, with which it increasingly overlaps, it is a violent place full of colorful characters and arcane lingo, of "naked shorts" and "pump 'n' dumps." And it specializes in creating illusions that are as complex as a Broadway play—and as simple as a game of three-card monte.

It was in this world that Albert Alain Chalem and Maier Lehmann lived— and died. The men, who were promoting stocks over the Internet together, were both shot in the head on October 25 and left to die on the marble floor in the $1.1 million home in Colts Neck, New Jersey, where Chalem lived.

Their world might seem arcane—except that its denizens bilk Americans out of roughly $2 billion a year, securities regulators say. The problem is so severe that regulators and prosecutors have made it one of their chief goals to crack down on what they used to dismiss as "penny-stock fraud," before it became clear that the money involved amounted to many billions of pennies.

"A sustained, prolonged bull market really does bring out the crustaceans from the bottom of the sea," said Richard H. Walker, director of enforcement for the Securities and Exchange Commission. "They're attracted to the money."

While the enforcement effort has closed down many of the big brokerage operations that pushed shady stocks over the telephone, Walker said, many people who were kicked out of the securities business have moved their schemes into cyberspace. "That's where the action is now," he said.

And that is where Chalem and Lehmann were before they were killed. In addition to running a Web site, Chalem was trading stocks electronically, and may have had an account under an assumed name at a Manhattan firm called Harbor Securities. Investigators are examining whether he traded there, and if it was linked to his death.

From the very first, investigators have suspected that the slayings somehow involved the two men's financial dealings, rather than their personal lives. And, although the investigation remains in its early stages, law enforcement officials have clearly not changed their minds.

On the surface, Lehmann, 37, seems to have had the more troubled work history. He had pleaded guilty to mail fraud in an insurance scheme and settled civil securities-fraud charges. Before his death he told *Barron's* magazine that he had secretly worked at Patterson, Travis Inc., a small brokerage firm with a history of regulatory troubles; company officials said yesterday that they had no record of his having worked there.

In fact, Lehmann was more than willing to talk. He told reporters, regulators, prosecutors and, apparently, anyone who would listen about what he said were various schemes and swindles.

But it was Chalem, 41, who cast the longer shadow in the world of shady stocks, and it is Chalem who is increasingly the focus of investigators. He had worked at a brokerage firm, A. S. Goldmen & Company, that prosecutors contend was a criminal enterprise—a charge that the firm denies. He also worked secretly at a firm called Toluca Pacific Securities, according to several people who knew him. Toluca, which is defunct, had a long history of regulatory runins and had links to career felons and to organized crime.

Mobsters have increasingly turned up in stock swindles. In January, two men whom prosecutors said were tied to the Bonanno and Genovese crime families pleaded guilty to federal charges that they participated in a conspiracy to manipulate the stock of an Arizona company that owns a health club; the president of the company was convicted of related charges in May in Federal District Court in Manhattan.

In June, federal prosecutors in Brooklyn indicted a group they said included members of the Colombo crime family and an associate of the Bor organized crime group of Russian immigrants.

The men, who prosecutors said ran rogue brokerage firms that manipulated stock prices, were charged with conspiracy, securities fraud and money laundering; they pleaded not guilty.

Chalem was widely believed, in the penny stock world, to have dealings with Russian organized crime and to be "a protected guy," as one lawyer put it.

New information is coming to light about his activities in the weeks before his death. Last week, federal prosecutors served subpoenas to retrieve trading records, which may be linked to Chalem, from Harbor Securities, which catered to self-employed day traders. Heavy financial losses recently forced the firm to close.

Whether Chalem's trading had anything to do with his death remains unclear. What is clear is that he and Lehmann were more accustomed to being predators than to being prey in the dangerous world they inhabited.

THE PERFORMANCE: EVERYTHING
FAKE EXCEPT THE MONEY

Their alternative Wall Street is not a big place; its players, who all seem to know each other, cluster in just a few spots: San Diego and La Jolla in Southern

California, Boca Raton, Florida, Vancouver and New York, the ground zero of stock fraud.

To be successful, stock frauds must look a lot like legitimate deals. But in reality, they are elaborately choreographed performances, in which everything is fake except the money the audience will lose when the play is over.

Fraudulent companies issue fraudulent press releases touting fraudulent products; fake newsletters make fake recommendations about fake stocks; phantom investors make phantom trades to push up the price of these phantom stocks. A small claque in the audience may be tossing tomatoes, but these skeptics—known as short-sellers—can often be bought off by the show's producers.

Between them, Chalem and Lehmann seem to have played every possible role in such productions. Behind-the-scenes operators, they did business over cellular phones and computers, from so-called boiler rooms full of phones and fast-talking salesmen, and most recently, on the Internet.

To understand how thousands of Americans get taken in by these shows, it helps to know a little bit about the legitimate side of Wall Street—and about how the real thing differs from its evil twin, as described in court documents, in interviews with regulators and prosecutors, and in discussions with people in the stock business.

In the real Wall Street, new companies that want to raise money pay investment firms a fee to sell shares of stock. In the shady Wall Street, almost none of the money raised from investors goes to the company; rather, it lines the pockets of brokers and promoters and their pals. In one case analyzed by state regulators in Alabama, a New York company raised $12.5 million from investors; $11 million of that went to insiders and brokers.

In the real Wall Street, public companies are vetted by accountants and auditors and lawyers and investment firms, all of them supervised by regulators. Companies that have stock outstanding must file quarterly financial reports with the Securities and Exchange Commission, and keep investors informed of major changes in their businesses.

In the ersatz Wall Street, companies avoid filing regulatory reports—lying on such reports is a crime—and communicate almost entirely by news releases, the more hyperbolic the better. (Without admitting or denying wrongdoing, one Florida executive recently settled regulatory charges over his press releases. These falsely claimed that the Moscow Ministry of Finance and Walt Disney World were negotiating to buy his company's process for turning scrap tires into oil.)

At legitimate companies, insiders, like executives and directors, must report, publicly, any time they buy or sell their own stock. People who own even 5 percent of a company must also reveal that through filings.

In the fake Wall Street, insiders use false names and dummy accounts to hide the fact that they control almost all of a company's stock that is available for trading. In one regulatory case recently filed in Federal District Court in

Brooklyn, the SEC contends that a group of stock promoters controlled as much as 95 percent of the tradable shares in several companies.

Though the real stock market is a complicated place, particularly in the short run, over the long haul a company's stock price rises when investors are optimistic about its future sales and profits; the stock price falls when investors worry that the company's business is in trouble.

In the false Wall Street, a stock rises like Peter Pan in the stage play, not because he is thinking merry little thoughts, but because he is attached to a wire strung from the theater's rigging. (Aptly, these manipulated stocks are called rigs.)

The stage for these stocks is usually the OTC Bulletin Board, a trading network run by the National Association of Securities Dealers, which also runs Nasdaq. But unlike the real Nasdaq market, the bulletin board will trade the stock of almost any company, no matter how small, secretive or downright preposterous.

Regulators predict that more than half of the roughly 6,000 companies that were trading on the bulletin board last year will be removed by next June, under new rules that require them to file current financial statements with regulators.

The cast of characters includes the promoters, who are often stockbrokers barred from the securities business, their lawyers and public-relations advisers. The production also needs someone still in the securities business who can execute trades.

Other starring roles usually belong to corporate executives, who are mostly in on the rig, though sometimes they are innocents desperate to raise money for their companies.

And then there are short-sellers, who are people who bet that share prices will fall (and make a profit when that happens). In some cases, they are doing all they can to make sure the production is a flop.

The production may call on the brokers and cold-callers to unload shares on the public, although the Internet is making such brokers increasingly unnecessary; now, investors can be persuaded to buy stock electronically. "The Internet has put this type of fraud on steroids," said Cameron Funkhouser, vice president of market regulation for the National Association of Securities Dealers.

THE CHOREOGRAPHY: HYPED-UP
IDEAS, CONTROLLED STOCK

The plot of the play always begins with the company. The ideal stock-fraud company has some whiz-bang new product that will excite investors, like a self-chilling beer can, springy shoes for race horses, or a cure for baldness or for tooth decay. Also popular are gold mines in obscure locations, theme restaurants in Las Vegas and anything in cyberspace with a .com after it.

Sometimes the purported business will change in the course of the scheme; according to a ruling in a federal lawsuit, one outfit called Sky Scientific claimed at various times to be running gold mines, a financial services company and the first riverboat casino in Moscow. Occasionally the company is a small operation that has a real product, but it is just not as thrilling as the company's public relations makes out. (The vitamins do not really cure cancer; the Internet service has not really signed up every household in Peru.)

One company Lehmann was involved with, Electro-Optical Systems, claimed to be developing a computer gizmo that would read fingerprints, so that users could sign in without having to remember pesky passwords.

His original role was to hook up the would-be inventor of the product with the "investment bankers" who were supposedly raising money for the company, according to a decision in a lawsuit filed last year by the SEC in Federal District Court in Manhattan. The inventor was not named as a defendant in the case, which is now dormant while a criminal investigation continues. Lehmann settled the regulators' charges and paid $630,000 in fines and restitution.

The key, from the con artists' point of view, is to get control of the shares of stock, which might be called Act 1. Sometimes shady brokerage firms stage "initial public offerings," but a faster and cheaper method—the one Lehmann's group used—is to merge the company with a shell corporation, which has stock outstanding but no business.

Almost everyone involved in the scheme is paid with stock; the promoters usually control huge blocks in accounts with false names, often overseas.

They all make money by making the shares rise in price. They often do this in part by making fake trades at arbitrary prices. In the case of Electro-Optical, regulators contend that the promoters put in an order to buy shares at $7 each, far above the 20 cents for which shares had last changed hands before the promotion began.

Once the stock price has been pumped up, it is time to lure outsiders into buying the shares. Lehmann helped out with the public relations. He got an Internet newsletter to choose Electro-Optical as its "pick of the year"; the newsletter's owner was later sued by the SEC, which accused him of secretly taking stock and cash from companies in exchange for recommending their stocks; he is contesting the charges.

Lehmann also approved a press release that claimed, falsely, that Electro-Optical had just received a big order for its products. (Neither order nor products existed.) Investors, entranced with the concept and the rising stock price, began to buy the inflated stock.

After the pump comes the dump. Those in the know sell their shares to unsuspecting investors. Lehmann had received 100,000 shares, for which he paid nothing and which he put in an account in his wife's name; when he sold, he made about half a million dollars. All told, regulators say, those involved in the Electro-Optical rigging made $12 million by dumping their shares.

Once the promoters stop pumping the stock, its price usually plunges. Anyone who wants to buy Electro-Optical today can get 10 shares for a penny.

BAILING OUT: SPECIAL HANDLING FOR SHORT SELLERS

Some inventive stock promoters find a way to make money on the falling price, too, by selling short. To do this, a short seller simply borrows some shares from a brokerage house, promising to replace them later, and then sells them. If the trader has guessed right and the stock's price later falls, he can replace the borrowed shares—a step known as "covering"—by buying shares at the new, lower price.

His profit is the difference between the price at which he sold the borrowed shares and the price at which he bought the replacements. But if the share price rises, he can easily lose his entire investment.

While short selling can be a legitimate practice, it can also be abused. Chalem's friends and former business allies say he practiced a more aggressive form of short-selling, called naked shorting. Brokerage houses that deal in a particular stock can short it without borrowing the shares first. Going through those cooperative brokers, speculators like Chalem sell, and sell and sell— thereby guaranteeing that the stock's price will plummet.

A year or two ago, Chalem's associates say, he was shorting the stock of the Quigley Corporation of Doylestown, Pennsylvania, which makes zinc lozenges that it says relieve common colds. The company blamed short-sellers for the decline in its stock, which has dropped from $23 in the fall of 1997 to about $3 today. Skeptics said the company's share price was too high and, indeed, sales of the lozenges have been falling.

But a debate over the true merits of most penny stocks is pointless; in many cases, both the promoters and the short sellers know that the stocks are rigged. Then, the question is simply who has enough power—and money—to prevail in what is really trench warfare.

Promoters may try to make short-sellers go away by giving them free shares that the short-sellers can use to cover and close out their positions with big profits. This has caused some prosecutors to believe that this sort of short-selling is really a kind of extortion, though that is hard to prove.

Both sides use rough tactics in their efforts to win. They try to plant stories in the press. They call regulators and prosecutors to inform on each other.

And they threaten each other with physical harm, backed up by visits from burly men. John Fiero, a prominent short seller and president of the firm Fiero Brothers in Manhattan, has repeatedly complained to the police about the threats he has received.

And that violence may ultimately be the biggest difference between the real Wall Street and the parallel universe inhabited by people like Chalem and Lehmann.

Real Wall Street takes a lot of financial risks. But the crooked Wall Street "is not just a financially dangerous world," said Stephen Luparello, a senior vice president of the N.A.S.D. "It's also a physically dangerous world."

The New York Times, November 19, 1999
http://www.nytimes.com/library/financial/111999broker-deaths.html

CRITICAL THINKING QUESTIONS

1. Are penny stocks a wise investment? Why, or why not?
2. What agency or agencies should regulate penny stocks, and how should they regulate them?
3. How could brokerage firms or individuals manipulate stock prices?
4. How has the Internet influenced penny stocks? How will this influence change in the future?

STORY-SPECIFIC QUESTIONS

1. Most may not know it, but there are really two Wall Streets. What are these two Wall Streets?
2. In the shady Wall Street, what happens to the money raised from investors in a new company?
3. In the ersatz Wall Street, companies avoid filing regulatory reports because lying on such reports is a crime, but how do these companies communicate?
4. Where are these manipulated stocks generally traded?
5. Briefly explain selling short.

SHORT APPLICATION ASSIGNMENTS

1. In teams or individually, answer the story-specific questions; keep your answers to 25–75 words for each question.
2. In teams of three to five persons each, or as a whole class, discuss your responses to the critical thinking questions.
3. Prepare a one-page memo report (200–250 words) to your instructor in which you summarize this article. You will find a model one-page report on the Web site (nytimes.swcollege.com).
4. Write an executive summary (200–250 words). As an administrative assistant to a busy executive, you are expected to summarize selected articles and present important points. You will find a model executive summary on the Web site.
5. Summarize this article (100–125 words) for your company's newsletter. You will find a model newsletter article on the Web site.
6. Individually or in groups, explore the Securities and Exchange Commission Web site (http://www.sec.gov/). What areas of the SEC site would deal with securities fraud? Which other regulatory organizations are linked to this Web site? Your instructor may ask you to present your findings in an oral report or submit a 150- to 200-word summary.

7. Individually or in groups, explore the National Association of Securities Dealers regulation Web site (http://www.nasdr.com/). What resources does this site offer an investor? Your instructor may ask you to present your findings in an oral report or submit a 150- 200-word summary.

BUILDING RESEARCH SKILLS:

1. Individually or in teams, explore three of the following Web sites: The National Association of Securities Dealers (http://www.nasd.com/), Nasdaq Stock Market (http://www.nasdaq.com), Nasdaq UK (http://www.nasdaq-amex-uk.com/), Securities and Exchange Commission (http://www.sec.gov/), American Stock Exchange (http://www.amex.com) and New York Stock Exchange (http://www.nyse.com). What regulatory information do they contain? What regulatory power do they hold? Your instructor may ask you to submit a three- to five-page essay, post a Web page or report your results in a five-minute presentation, along with a letter of transmittal explaining your findings.

2. Using at least three other references (e.g., books, research-journal articles, newspaper or magazine stories or credible Web sites), write an 800- to 1,000-word essay that addresses two of the critical thinking questions offered earlier. Assume that your essay will be used as an internal reference for a financial institution's corporate investment guidelines.

3. Using at least three other references (e.g., books, research-journal articles, newspaper or magazine stories or credible Web sites), post an 800- to 1,000-word Web page that addresses at least two of the earlier critical thinking questions. Assume that your page will be posted in the investment section of a corporate intranet.

Crash Course: Just What's Driving the Crisis in Emerging Markets?

By Louis Uchitelle

Davos, Switzerland—Among the movers and shakers gathered here for the World Economic Forum, a striking metaphor is helping to frame the debate over the global financial crisis that began in Asia and has spread to several other developing countries. The debacle, some say, brings to mind a slick stretch of highway, scene of a half-dozen recent auto accidents. So is it careless driving or the highway that is the cause of the accidents?

Substitute freewheeling worldwide capital flows and unrestricted lending for the slippery, fast-moving highway. Make South Korea, Thailand, Indonesia, Russia and Brazil stand-ins for the drivers and their cars. The accidents are the panics and recessions—the crackups—that have devastated each of these countries. And the question now so widely debated is simple enough: Are the countries mostly to blame or the unrestricted capital flows, or both?

After the first accidents, the countries came in for almost all the blame. It was because of crony capitalism, bad banking and overleveraged real estate investments, many experts said. Fix the sloppy financial practices and also make enough bailout money available when a country gets into trouble—basically the current strategy of the International Monetary Fund for Brazil—and the accidents will be avoided or, at worst, will be mere fender benders.

But spectacular wrecks have occurred with alarming frequency and severity in the last 18 months, even in Brazil, and some who had mostly blamed the countries have begun to argue, here and in earlier interviews, that the system needs serious fixing, too.

The Clinton administration had placed most of the blame on the countries, and still does. But its view, like that of the IMF, is starting to reflect a more nuanced appraisal. "We have seen that countries need to pursue sounder policies and avoid lurching for short-term capital, as Mexico and Thailand did," said Lawrence Summers, the deputy treasury secretary. But in a phone interview this week from Washington, he also called for "more prudence on the part of the lenders."

And in the administration's most direct acknowledgment so far that it is not necessarily always committed to unrestricted capital flows, he added: "Where countries have controls that restrict short-term lending, we have not in general sought to dismantle them."

Some on Wall Street are similarly shifting ground. "It is appropriate to certainly consider fixing the system," said Stephen Roach, chief economist at Morgan Stanley Dean Witter. Morgan Stanley normally makes more money when capital flows freely and the firm can lend where and how it sees best.

But the recent string of crackups has given Roach second thoughts. "I am not completely convinced that restrictions on the system are necessary," he said, "but unstable capital flows have clearly been a precipitant of these crises."

At the top of many lists for fixing the system are proposals to limit the flow of short-term foreign loans to developing countries, loans that often contributed to more rapid growth but which piled up in huge amounts in Asia, Russia and Brazil. Then, at the first hint of trouble, much of the money fled, precipitating and worsening a full-scale financial collapse.

But other systemwide suggestions are winning favor as well: pursing flexible exchange rates, for example, to avoid sudden, frightening devaluations; introducing bankruptcy laws that let companies deep in foreign debt borrow and resume operations even before they pay off the old debts; and standstill provisions in lending agreements that would temporarily prevent a foreign lender from withdrawing loans from a South Korea or a Brazil in the midst of a crisis.

What they have in common is an effort to put more of the burden on international banks and other lenders to evaluate risks more carefully early on and suffer more of the consequences later if things go bad.

"The banks don't like this; they value liquidity of lending," said Barry Eichengreen, an international economist at the University of California at Berkeley. "But if they had a provision in their loan agreements that they cannot pull out their money right away when a crisis is developing, maybe they would not lend the money in the first place."

Some experts now favor rules that prevent not only foreign lenders but wealthy nationals—Brazilians, for example—from canceling their short-term loans and investments, then converting this money from local currencies into dollars and taking the dollars out of the country. Wealthy Brazilians, many of them already moving chunks of capital abroad, hold more than $150 billion in their government's debt and rushing this money out of the country would quickly exhaust Brazil's dollar reserves.

"My view is that basically all short-term debt constitutes potential capital flight," said Paul Krugman, an economist at the Massachusetts Institute of Technology. "Brazil is at risk not only from foreign lenders, but from anyone who can take money out of the country."

Perhaps some of these measures would make the highway safer for ordinary drivers. But before the dangerous stretch of road is rebuilt in hopes of preventing future accidents, the smashed cars of the last 18 months have to be repaired and put back in operation. There is little agreement on how to do that. Rather there are two diametrically opposite, so far unyielding, approaches.

The current practice, carried out at the insistence of the Clinton administration and the IMF, is to require countries in trouble to adopt policies intended to limit devaluations of a country's currency and restore the confidence of international lenders. If currencies plunge too far, the argument goes, then foreign loans become much harder to repay and inflation sets in as imports shoot up in price.

"The mainstream view would still be that the key solutions to crises remain policy adjustments within the countries themselves," said William Cline, chief economist at the Institute for International Finance, which represents lenders. "Once you restore confidence in a country's financial system, then you can get its economy growing again."

The chief tools in this approach are sharply higher interest rates and cutbacks in public spending. But the high rates and spending cutbacks invariably produce recessions.

The Clinton administration argues that once confidence in a financial system is restored, interest rates can then come down, as they have in South Korea and Thailand, and nations can begin the long climb out of recession. But even Thailand and South Korea are still on the side of the road, their economies spinning their wheels rather than moving forward again.

"It is too facile to say, 'Look at Korea and Thailand, they are turning around,'" said Dani Rodrik, a Harvard economist. "Their economies have taken bigger hits than either country has experienced in the last 30 years."

Like the East Asian countries, Brazil, the latest victim of a financial panic, is hewing to policies that are plunging that country into recession. And as the hobbling of giant Brazil slows economic activity everywhere in Latin America, the odds rise that even the United States and Europe could be caught in the spreading global crisis.

That would not happen so much because of recession in Latin America, but because some new blow—a major bankruptcy, for example, or a sharp decline in American stock prices—undermines confidence in an American financial system still nervous about Asia and Brazil.

The contrasting view is argued most vehemently by Jeffrey Sachs of Harvard, who insists that high interest rates and austerity measures are bringing disaster to many emerging markets. He would keep interest rates down to encourage economic activity and let exchange rates find their own level. A growing economy is more likely to restore investor confidence, he says, than a recessionary one burdened by high interest rates.

"The Treasury and the IMF have driven a large part of the developing world into recession," said Sachs, who directs Harvard's Institute for International Development. "And the Brazil case makes absolutely clear that the first step is not to defend overvalued currencies. The punishing cost of this is overwhelmingly high. This is a lesson that the IMF and the Treasury have continued to ignore. I don't understand why."

For all the disagreement over how to repair the damaged East Asian and Latin economies, much of the debate centers not on the present, but on how to avoid financial crises in the future. And here the proposals increasingly involve a mixture of fixing the system and fixing the countries—repairing the highway and making the drivers more cautious and skilled.

On the country side, several proposals have been made to set up a super central bank that would make huge amounts of money available to bail out a country in the event of a crisis. George Soros, the speculator and philanthropist, has offered one version, and another comes from Stanley Fischer, the IMF's first deputy managing director. But to qualify for such bailouts in the future, the countries would have to strengthen their banking and financial systems.

"You would shore up the international system by providing a more meaningful lender of last resort," said C. Fred Bergsten, director of the Institute for International Economics.

Those who focus mostly on the system would require, among other things, that banks put aside extra money in a reserve fund if they lent into emerging countries heavily burdened with foreign debt. "Putting aside money in that fashion reduces the profitability of a loan, which in turn makes lenders more cautious," said Ricardo French-Davis, a Chilean economist who works in Santiago with the U.N. Economic Commission for Latin America.

Krugman of MIT goes further in blaming the system and in arguing that the need to fix structural problems in individual countries should not stand in the way of broader macro-economic measures, particularly those designed to stimulate growth in hard times.

In the current issue of *Foreign Affairs*, he writes that over the last 25 years, much of the global economy has returned in many ways to a "pre-Depression free-market capitalism," with its virtues but also its vices—the main vice being a vulnerability to spectacular crackups.

"It is hard to avoid concluding that sooner or later we will have to turn the clock at least part of the way back," he writes. "To limit capital flows for countries that are unsuitable for either currency unions or free floating; to reregulate financial markets to some extent; and to seek low, but not too low, inflation rather than price stability. We must heed the lessons of Depression economics, lest we be forced to relearn them the hard way."

The New York Times, January 29, 1999
http://www.nytimes.com/library/world/global/012999econ-crises.html

CRITICAL THINKING QUESTIONS

1. Is borrowing from the International Monetary Fund the best avenue a country should take when facing financial problems? Why, or why not?
2. Are the countries mostly to blame for their internal financial panics and recessions? Are they to blame for unrestricted capital flows? Should they be blamed for both?
3. What is your opinion of the strategies suggested for avoiding an international financial collapse?
4. Why are economists cautious about establishing a "super bank" to bail nations out of dire financial straits?
5. Is it better raise or lower interest rates in order restore investor confidence in a country? Explain.

STORY-SPECIFIC QUESTIONS

1. What did the experts cite as the causes of the multinational financial crisis that began in mid-1997?
2. What is at the top of many lists for fixing the global financial system?
3. What other suggestions for repairing the global financial system are winning favor?
4. What are the chief tools to limit devaluations of a country's currency and restore the confidence of international lenders? What are the consequences of these tools?
5. Briefly explain the contrasting view held by Jeffrey Sachs of Harvard.

SHORT APPLICATION ASSIGNMENTS

1. In teams or individually, answer the story-specific questions; keep your answers to 25–75 words for each question.
2. In teams of three to five persons each, or as a whole class, discuss your responses to the critical thinking questions.
3. Prepare a one-page memo report (200–250 words) to your instructor in which you summarize this article. You will find a model one-page report on the Web site (nytimes.swcollege.com).
4. Write an executive summary (200–250 words). As an administrative assistant to a busy executive, you are expected to summarize selected articles and present important points. You will find a model executive summary on the Web site.
5. Summarize this article (100–125 words) for your company's newsletter. You will find a model newsletter article on the Web site.
6. Read one of the additional stories in *The New York Times on the Web* special section on The World Financial Crisis (http://www.nytimes.com/library/financial/index-global-fin-crisis.html). Your instructor may ask you to present the story in an oral report or submit a 150- to 200-word summary.
7. Individually or in teams, research the Web site of International Monetary Fund (http://www.imf.int/) or World Bank Web (http://www.worldbank.org/). Who sponsors this organization? What services does it offer? How is it funded? Your instructor may ask you to present the story in an oral report or submit a 150- to 200-word summary.

BUILDING RESEARCH SKILLS

1. Individually or in teams, research the concept and role of the International Monetary Fund (http://www.imf.int/) and World Bank Web (http://www.worldbank.org/). Based upon the information you gather, explain why each system is necessary for guarding against serious currency depreciation in the exchange markets. Your instructor may ask you to submit a three- to five-page essay, post a Web page or report your results in a five-minute presentation, along with a letter of transmittal explaining your essay.

2. Individually or in teams, read at least three of the additional stories in *The New York Times on the Web* special section on The World Financial Crisis (http://www. nytimes.com/library/financial/index-global-fin-crisis.html). Your instructor may ask you to submit a three- to five-page essay, post a Web page or report your summary of these stories in a five-minute presentation, along with a letter of transmittal explaining your summary.

3. Using at least three other references (e.g., books, research-journal articles, newspaper or magazine stories or credible Web sites), write an 800- to 1,000-word essay that addresses two of the critical thinking questions offered earlier. Assume that your essay will be used as an internal reference for a financial institution's corporate investment guidelines.

4. Using at least three other references (e.g., books, research-journal articles, newspaper or magazine stories or credible Web sites), post an 800- to 1,000-word Web page that addresses at least two of the earlier critical thinking questions. Assume that your page will be posted in the investment section of a corporate intranet.

Banking 101: The Smaller the Fry, the Hotter the Pan

By Timothy L. O'Brien

Last weekend, I deposited a fat six-figure sum into my checking account. The windfall, alas, was from the sale of my home, not from my weekly paycheck at *The New York Times*, where for the past several weeks I have been writing about a major money laundering investigation.

It was the single biggest bank deposit I have ever made and the sleuths at Chase Manhattan took notice right away. Their system rejected my deposit.

On Wednesday, a very nice, very harried, branch manager called to tell me the deposit was too large for my account. Moreover, the account was only in my name and the checks were made out to me and my wife. Set up a new account or take your money elsewhere, advised the manager.

Banks are supposed to do this. After all, how do the folks at Chase know where I got all that money from? Still, I was amused. How did billions of dollars from Russia—*billions*—zip through a handful of accounts at the Bank of New York for almost two years without anyone taking notice?

Paper checks deposited in a local branch are pretty easy for banks to track. But much of the money flowing around the world these days flits across borders electronically in the blink of an eye. And that can be much harder for banks to monitor.

Bank of New York, which is now entangled in the biggest money laundering investigation in history, processes billions of dollars of transactions a day. Understandably, a lot of money could sneak by unnoticed when there's that much passing through. But at least $3 billion slipped through just nine accounts at the Bank of New York between 1996 and 1998, right before the Federal Bureau of Investigation marched in to examine all that activity.

Think of it this way: A python swallows a frog and nobody notices the frog is missing. Then the python swallows a rabbit: Not a lot of guess-work here because you can see where the poor rabbit is—it's stuck right in the middle of the python.

When an obscure operation called the Benex Corporation deposited billions of dollars of Russian funds into accounts at the Bank of New York it looked like the python swallowed a pig—yet despite the tremendous bulge in Benex's accounts, nobody at the bank examined it closely.

In contrast, alarm bells started ringing about Benex and related accounts at Republic Bank in August 1998, just one month after the bank installed a new system to monitor wire transfers. The heavy traffic in the accounts concerned Republic, which alerted Federal officials immediately. In the new era of looser financial regulation, banks are expected to be the first line of defense against criminals. Essentially, this requires them to be vigilant and know the backgrounds of their customers. If something about an account makes them suspicious, banks are required to notify regulators right away.

Bank of New York's chief executive, Thomas A. Renyi, acknowledged in recent Congressional testimony that the bank failed to supervise the Benex accounts effectively. That lapse will be a matter for regulators to address. Beyond that, however, it is not clear whether the bank did anything illegal.

The exact sources of some $7.5 billion that moved through Benex accounts at the Bank of New York between 1996 and 1999 are still unknown and the bank has not been charged with wrongdoing. Other than Renyi's testimony, the bank has largely declined to comment except to say it is cooperating with the Federal investigation.

Moreover, the mass of investigators swarming around the case face enormous hurdles unraveling the traffic through the Benex accounts and proving that sources of the funds were tainted.

Money laundering refers to the criminal practice of taking ill-gotten gains, or "dirty" money, and filtering them through a sequence of bank accounts so they are "cleaned" to look like legitimate profits from legal activities. Exposing this process, however, is daunting.

"It's difficult to prosecute money laundering because disproportionate activity in an account doesn't mean you have money laundering," said Mark D. Seltzer, an attorney with Goulston & Storrs in Boston, and a former Federal prosecutor. "You have to prove that the source of the money that created this activity in your accounts was ill-gotten gains from specific criminal activities."

One of the most high-profile financial fraud prosecutions in recent years, the 1991 case against the Bank of Credit and Commerce International that was spearheaded by Manhattan District Attorney Robert M. Morgenthau, did not result in convictions of two of the most notable defendants in the case, the Washington power broker Clark M. Clifford and his protégé, Robert A. Altman.

But many in the legal community view Morgenthau's prosecution of B.C.C.I. as a landmark success because it unraveled an illegal financial scheme clearly operating beyond the pale and helped force the payment of more than $1.5 billion in fines.

"If you just look at the criminal prosecution, it obviously wasn't successful," said Robert E. Powis, a former deputy assistant secretary for enforcement at the U.S. Treasury. "But they helped shut the apparatus down and they did get heavy fines disgorged and that's another measure of success."

But B.C.C.I. was a rogue bank. At worst, based on what has surfaced so far, the Bank of New York may have had a troubled operation inside its walls, but no one in the banking community has ever considered it to be a rogue bank. The comparison with B.C.C.I., then, lies elsewhere.

"The relevance of the B.C.C.I. matter is that it demonstrated the difficulties of prosecuting these kinds of cases," said Harry W. Albright Jr., the court-appointed trustee of First American, a bank once controlled by B.C.C.I. "It is very difficult to unravel banking cases these days because of their international scope. There is no quick fix because the cases require cooperation across borders."

In other words, the ultimate answers to the questions swirling around the Bank of New York can only be found in Russia. And getting real cooperation from the Russians in the Bank of New York case may be the biggest hurdle American investigators face.

The New York Times, October 3, 1999
http://www.nytimes.com/library/review/100399money-laundering-review.html

CRITICAL THINKING QUESTIONS

1. Should banks refuse to accept certain deposits? Why, or why not?
2. In the new era of looser financial regulation, should banks be expected to be the first line of defense against criminals? Why, or why not?
3. Why do some countries have lax controls concerning money laundering?
4. Why do some countries pride themselves on secret banking accounts?
5. What *could* be done to prevent money laundering?
6. What *should* be done to prevent money laundering?

STORY-SPECIFIC QUESTIONS

1. What two reasons did Chase Manhattan give for rejecting the author's deposit?
2. Why may it be hard for banks to monitor much of the money flowing around the world these days?
3. How much money slipped through just nine accounts at the Bank of New York between 1996 and 1998?
4. What is money laundering?

SHORT APPLICATION ASSIGNMENTS

1. In teams or individually, answer the story-specific questions; keep your answers to 25–75 words for each question.
2. In teams of three to five persons each, or as a whole class, discuss your responses to the critical thinking questions.
3. Prepare a one-page memo report (200–250 words) to your instructor in which you summarize this article. You will find a model one-page report on the Web site (nytimes.swcollege.com).
4. Write an executive summary (200–250 words). As an administrative assistant to a busy executive, you are expected to summarize selected articles and present important points. You will find a model executive summary on the Web site.

5. Summarize this article (100–125 words) for your company's newsletter. You will find a model newsletter article on the Web site.
6. Read "Grand Jury Indicts Fugitive Financier on Fraud and Other Charges" (http://www.nytimes.com/library/financial/100899frankel-indict.html). Your instructor may ask you to present the story in an oral report or submit a 150- to 200-word summary.

BUILDING RESEARCH SKILLS

1. Individually or in teams, read at least three of the additional "Russian Money Laundering" articles linked from this story. Your instructor may ask you to submit a three- to five-page essay, post a Web page or report your summary of these stories in a five-minute presentation, along with a letter of transmittal explaining your summary.
2. Obtain a copy and read *The Lexus and the Olive Tree* by Thomas L. Friedman. Write an overview (800–1,000 words) of its central thesis.
3. Using at least three other references (e.g., books, research-journal articles, newspaper or magazine stories or credible Web sites), write an 800- to 1,000-word essay that addresses two of the critical thinking questions offered earlier. Assume that your essay will be used as an internal reference for a financial institution's corporate investment guidelines.
4. Using at least three other references (e.g., books, research-journal articles, newspaper or magazine stories or credible Web sites), post an 800- to 1,000-word Web page that addresses at least two of the earlier critical thinking questions. Assume that your page will be posted in the investment section of a corporate intranet.